Beginning to Manage

Brian van Deventer

EME Ministries
PO Box 73004
Ano Glyfada 16510
Greece

ISBN # 1-931178-12-7

FOR ORDERING INFORMATION, PLEASE CONATCT:

VISION PUBLISHING
1115 D STREET, RAMONA CALIFORNIA
www.visionpublishingservices.com
1-800-9-VISION

Dedication:

To two women to have showed me that management is neither a masculine nor feminine affair, but one of competence:

My mother, who has managed more people and diverse situations through the years, sometimes willingly and other times out of necessity. She has done this tirelessly at her places of work, while still managing at home; and I can think of few tougher places to deal with personalities and preferences than in the home.

Dr. Gail Stathis, my co-worker and my pastor. She has modeled for me what it is to manage on behalf of others, even in the most trying of times; and, what it is to manage an office of one's own responsibility and concerns. More than simply modeling what is right, she has always been honest, forthright and open about what is not right, and therefore not working. This vulnerability and openness has been invaluable to the learning process, and has been offered at great risk.

Thank you.

Contents

Introduction to the Management Series

There are many texts available regarding the topic of management and its related subjects, so as in any effort like this one, the question must be asked, why another one? What can be presented in the following pages so different from what I may find elsewhere? The answer to that question may surprise you (or not): "nothing." We are not so bold as to claim to add something *new*, but hopefully something *purposeful* nonetheless.

What do we mean by such a statement? We mean that, in this series of books, we are attempting to take principles already known and taught by many, compile them into a useful set of teachings, and use them to train and encourage us to be more diligent in our approach to life-work. Simply put, to be better at what we do. So the goal is not novelty, but relevance. We hope to be able to supply you with some of the best thoughts on the subjects involved here, and to make it interesting, provocative and effective in training.

A note about the format of the books in this series: the thoughts contained herein are garnered from a wide variety of sources. Most, if not all of them, may be attributed to an equal variety of different authors and sources. A bibliography and works cited page of many of these sources is given at the conclusion of the texts. We recognize, however, that the list may be incomplete and that some of our notes may have been developed and entered into the text without the knowledge of its point of origin. In that case, we offer our apologies to the wise originators of those thoughts, and thank them for adding quality to our work.

Books in the series include:

- ***Beginning to Manage***
- ***Building by Team***
- ***Diverse Cultures, Diverse Leaders***
- ***Guideposts to Leadership: Into a New Day***
- ***Keeping Account: Basic Bookkeeping***
- ***Managing Change***
- ***Organizational Communication***
- ***Organizing for Quality***
- ***Projects and Plans***
- ***Start Right, Finish Strong: A guide to coaching and mentoring***
- ***The Greatest Resource: Human Resource Management***

Beginning to Manage

This book is designed to introduce the new student of management to some of the basic principles of tried and true experience in the discipline. For the well traveled, well worn manager, it may be a simple and welcome refresher, or even a challenge to some of his or her own perceptions of leadership and management.

Certainly, the level of experience of the individual is a relevant consideration when approaching this book. It does not challenge the relevance, however. What we are seeking to discover are principles that can help to guide the way that we do the work of management, which we all know to be quite the challenge. (Or, will find out to be the case as we get into it!)

The task is set out before us. This is an introductory text on basic management concepts, principles and practices. It includes approaches to traditional management functions of planning, organizing, leading and controlling. It places some focus on management applications at workplace and in everyday situations. Our hope is to accomplish some basic goals: 1) to understand management concepts in order to become a knowledgeable and effective employee or manager, 2) to apply the principles to the workplace in order to perform managerial tasks better or view business issues from a management perspective so as to get along with managers better, 3) to improve skills to manage professional and personal lives, which is a universal need, 4) to better plan and organize activities, motivate and influence others as well as monitor environments to succeed in both professional and family living, and 5) to acquire the tools necessary to transfer knowledge of management principles in a teaching environment.

Because this is an introductory text, many of the principles contained here are reexamined, strengthened and built upon in the subsequent books of this series.

A note about the use of gender in this book may help the reader to follow the flow of the text. Male and female pronouns have been used interchangeably in order to stress the equal application of the principles to both genders, and to avoid an endless use of he/she compounds. In no way is the use of one or the other pronoun intended to indicate a particular application of the principle to the indicated gender, nor to exclude the other, unless that fact is very clearly stated within the text.

Chapter 1
Management 101

Brent was the best and brightest in his MBA course. He had learned the latest techniques, studied the charts and graphs, and absorbed countless testimonies from some of the world's top executives. Surely, he knew what it was going to take to perform well as he studied all of the bullet points in expensive textbooks in order to ace his tests. He subscribed to the best management periodicals and made sure that his library contained the classics. He could dress the part, speak comfortably to a crowd and write with ease.

Leaving school, Brent was grabbed by a reputable company to begin his march through middle management. It wouldn't be long before more of the rungs of the ladder of success were below him than above him.

He knew so much more than others working in his office. Some had never even been to school. For others, academia was so long ago, it could only be assumed that their learning was outdated. As for the rest, well if they were as good as Brent, they would be occupying his office, now wouldn't they. He was indispensable, brought in to do a job. Recruited to get things in line; to activate new policies and procedures. It was time to get this machine oiled and running smoothly so that the bosses upstairs could take notice of his great talents and advance him into greater responsibilities. The day of reckoning had arrived.

But Brent forgot one fundamental fact—if indeed he had ever learned it in the beginning. His job was not going to be about knowing better than those around him. It was not going to be about showing every worker another level of expertise. In this office, at this time, Brent would be called upon for a different role: that of coach. That of counselor. Brent was hired to be a motivator and encourager; he was called upon to find the way to draw the best from his workers, not to tell them how to proceed.

Welcome to today's world of management.

The key to this book is obviously (and hopefully!) to learn the principles of effective management, without getting so bogged down in the process that it is impossible to remember, no less put into action, the principles learned. Management 101 is about engaging the basics: essential elements of management skills and the beginnings of leadership development.

Equally obvious is that, since you have come far enough to obtain this material, you are either involved in the tasks of management now, or you are planning to be placed in that position in the (perhaps not-so-distant) future. So, welcome to the pursuit! In the next few moments, we are going to explore together some of the essentials to fulfill your *calling* as a manager.

Why do we say, "calling"? Because in order to reach the point of entering that management position you have either demonstrated skills and abilities (dare we call them "gifts"?) that have propelled or elevated you to this point, or you have created something of your own that requires you now to care for your creation. In either case, it is time to come to grips with the task of becoming the motivator, encourager, builder and promoter of that task to which you now find yourself entrusted.

Some who have studied management before may have some red flags rising already. This is because we have already used terms above that some would relate more to "leadership" than to "management". For a long time, especially in Leadership Studies, we have learned that there is quite a difference between leadership and management—and in that context there is. It will be our contention, however, that management in the new century and beyond (or at least until the social and educational cycles of learning come around again) does, and will, require more leadership from managers than ever before. The days of the functionary manager have ended. Bring on the leaders!

> **"Both management and leadership are needed to make teams and organizations successful. Trying to decide which is more important is like trying to decide whether the right or left wing is more important to an airplane's flight. I'll take both please!"**
>
> **-- Jim Clemmer**

It's a privilege!

What a concept! You are privileged as a manager to be in the position of one with great influence in and over the lives of those working with you. The decisions that you take, the way that you communicate, the environment that you promote will have an unavoidable and acute influence in the every day lives of your employees and coworkers; that is, the experiences of the work day, as well as the impact of those experiences upon their life outside of the office.

You are in a position to be a servant of benefit and blessing in the lives of those working for you, if you so choose to be. You are equally in a position to be the envoy of stress, hardship and potential failure. The choices that you make as a manager will be profound, for it is left to you to be the *manager* of the environment as well as the people and the workload. It is a heavy cross to carry, if that is the choice that you will embrace. As the responsibility mounts, however, so too will the rewards.

Few others will have such a profound part to play in the situations of those working with them. The success of that which you are a part and the welfare of those playing their own parts in the process is in many ways down to you. It's a privilege indeed, which leads us to understand that there are good approaches, and bad ones, that will influence the way that we manage and lead.

It's an attitude!

This privilege leads us to grapple with the kind of person that is "manager material". The simple fact is that, as we go through the outline of the management task, we will realize that much of it is simple logic. A thoughtful person should always be able to manage, it would seem. But as many of us have learned before, *knowing* something and actually *doing* something can be two separate themes entirely. As one of my friends in the quality management business likes to say, "It is the processes and procedures that make the difference. Not the knowledge." Many people learn the principles of effective management, but few may actually apply them.

To move training into practice requires the right skills, yes, but it also requires the right attitude. A true manager will see the betterment of people, procedures, and ultimately the business as the goals of their enterprise. You can find many helpful outlines and job descriptions of the true manager, but three stand out to us at this point that deserve to be shared in our recognition that managing is a privilege. They should be:

- **People-oriented.** The person with no interest in those working with or for him really has no place in the realm of management. For reasons already stated, and many more to come, the manager must be able to put people at the forefront of their decision making: workers, customers and clients, as well as bosses and shareholders. Listening, engaging, sometimes debating, determining and guiding will be unavoidable enterprises of the manager. He must work with people.

- **Pursuit-oriented.** One must be able to self-motivate, and then motivate others toward beneficial goals. These goals will be both personal and corporate. For instance, the true manager must be interested in education- the never ending process of learning to do better. Leading others to be interested in constant development and betterment can only be done by the person who is herself interested in the same. The hunger for learning and advancement will be central to her ability to manage well.

- **Practice-oriented.** There is an unprecedented amount of literature, training and quick-help material available in the realm of management and leadership today. The temptation is to become attuned to all of the latest fads and flavors in the management industry, chasing one set of tools after another without ever stopping to implement any of them in particular. Continual learning is essential, but not at the expense of *doing* something with that learning on occasion! The manager must be able to bring into the realm of practice all of that which has been absorbed through courses, seminars and conferences.

As in anything really worthwhile, shortcuts, as much as we like them, do not work in management. Developing the attitudes required for good management requires time and attention. Believing that one is already arrived at the place of complete competence will always leave that one at exactly that same place. The pieces of the personal puzzle are always developing, always evolving. We can always get better.

> **Good leaders make people feel that they're at the very heart of things, not at the periphery. Everyone feels that he or she makes a difference to the success of the organization. When that happens people feel centered and that gives their work meaning.**
>
> **– Warren G. Bennis**

The development of positive attitude in the workplace is a never ending work in progress. And it begins with the manager. The "firm hand" manager will need to find ways in certain circumstances to soften her stance a little. The "soft heart" manager will need, at times, to fortify herself, buckle up and take some harsher measures. The excellent managers will find their balance between the extremes.

The real job of the manager will not be to manipulate the constant workflow and production of his coworkers. It will be to serve as an example and an inspiration to others to be constantly developing, achieving and excelling. He will understand that, when employees are functioning well, they should be left to function. They should be encouraged to make their productive way through the workdays, with as little unnecessary interference as possible, and with as much freedom as can be created and allowed to further the corporate goals. He will see that the task of removing the negative and unnecessary from the mix will be more important in the end than trying to insert the superfluous (albeit good!) extras. The following chart gives some good characteristics for review in this regard.

The manager will seek to:	And to replace them with:
• Eliminate bad policies and procedures in the workplace. • Discourage poor treatment of coworkers and negative competition. • Minimize organizational or systematic weaknesses. • Remove the obstacles to creative, thoughtful activity.	• A solid and harmonious atmosphere in the workplace. • Support and encouragement of employees and coworkers • Including the appropriate training for excellence in their endeavors. • Challenged and improved systems, policies and procedures of the organization, at least within his realm of influence.

In the end, it's the people that benefit the work of the organization, and it is the organizations and their leadership who learn this fact that eventually excel. It is tempting, especially as task-oriented people (which managers often are), to see the workers as the problem to be managed rather than to see them as the resources available to help solve the problems and challenges of the workplace!

It's an enterprise!

As I was preparing this rather introductory section, an image of my own past came to mind. I could entitle the illustration, "On Horses and the Like", as it springs from my very short days as a rancher on the range of South Dakota (in the USA). Awe-inspiring vistas of endless pasture land (or, some would say endless tedium of boring, treeless terrain) became my playground for a few months of roping and riding. Working with both cattle and horses, I learned something interesting: corral-ing cattle is much easier than rounding horses (at least for the novices like myself).

In more managerial terms, coordinating the resources of a cattle drive is a simpler task than that with horses. Slower, less intelligent, less maneuverable and, frankly, less majestic, cattle are more inclined to move toward the point you direct them. A good whip and a loud voice will go far to achieving the purpose. (A fact held dear by many trying to be managers, unfortunately.) Horses, which are faster, more mobile and far more interested their freedom it would seem, make rounding them into one place and moving them in a single direction more challenging. I stumbled upon a solution.

Horses are inclined to follow a leader: that one beast that runs faster, kicks or bites harder, and ultimately holds sway over the others. I discovered that by coercing that lead horse (or instigating a chase, as the case may be!) into going where I wanted him to go would inspire the others to do so as well. And how could that be done? Get in front of him, and go. Lead by example, out front and center.

The lesson learned? I believe that people are more like horses than cattle. Cattle can be grouped, directed and moved. This is our more traditional view of management. Get the pieces assembled together, formulate the confines of their activity—through systems, processes, procedures, and job descriptions—and manage them forward in a common direction. *Horses, however, must be led rather moved.*

This is the enterprise of management: the coordination of freedom-loving creatures. (Some, admittedly, who love their freedom more than others.) This is especially true when your department is home to the best and the brightest that the company or the industry has to offer. A complete entourage of people with the capabilities to get certain jobs done, to play specific parts in the completion of tasks and projects, is placed in your hands. And now, as the manager, your job has shifted from that of being handed the resources to do a competent job to providing others with the resources they need to play their parts, while coordinating the many parts into a whole. You are in this position because, in all likelihood, you were proven to be capable in one or many of these particular tasks. But now, you must think above the individual tasks to see the end. You must identify the lead horses and get them to move. And you must help them to get their herds to move along with them as well. (No part of the above analogy should be taken to imply that we think of people as animals!)

The tools necessary for doing something yourself versus getting others to do those tasks are quite different. The transition is something that bears highlighting. From the daily environment of getting the appropriate resources, structuring them into an activity and producing a result, you are now being required to plan, organize, lead and follow up the various activities of others. A new preparation is required.

Our heading in this section describes this managerial activity as an "enterprise." The Cambridge Online Dictionary defines enterprise as "an organization, a difficult and important plan", as well as "eagerness to do something new and clever, despite any risks". I like both of these aspects in reference to the topic of management, because the last couple of decades have brought about a shift in thinking away from the boss/employee relationship to that of team and common enterprise. The old school thought highly of more hierarchical structures, but that model is breaking down in almost all realms of organization. Managers who are unwilling to take on the difficult and important task of coordinating people and tasks in new and clever ways, despite the risks, are bound to be left behind.

The old system was perhaps simpler, but less dynamic. In that paradigm, the traditional manager's task was more functionary; less leadership-oriented. Essentially, it was to:

- Divide and compartmentalize tasks.
- Assign those tasks to individuals in some organized fashion.
- Monitor those tasks, and motivate activity with carrots and sticks.
- Bring in the product or result on time, and under budget.

Today's growing paradigm still contains the same tasks, but from a very different perspective. The shifts in culture and social fabric have found their way into the cubicles and walled offices, the production lines and warehouse floors, around the business world. These changing values have caused more studious managers to see that their primary tasks have shifted from the defining of jobs and scrutiny of progress to that of formulating workspace and mental space that allows "coworkers" (rather than "employees") to behave creatively and responsibly. Patronage has given way to partnership.

Some may ask, "Can we continue to operate under the old model?" Sure. All things are possible. But consider the result. As the best and brightest begin to look for ways to cooperate at work, to collaborate and to create, they will move toward environments that promote such behavior. We have all heard the voices telling us that especially young, dynamic workers are no longer choosing jobs on the basis of location and pay scale alone, but also on the criteria of environment, freedom and fulfillment within the market place. They do not want to function as performers alone, but as partners in the vision. What will that leave you, then? The functionaries; those who simply work and exist; the work force drones. Some who will do a great job at the tasks assigned to them, others who will simply fill the function to the degree that is required. Words like "innovation," "challenge," "creativity," and "energy" will be of little use to you. The bottom line expectation will be your end product, while other companies or organizations are reaching for higher goals.

It's freedom... with responsibility!

In the organization that I help to lead, we often call upon the mantra, "freedom with responsibility." The managerial position described above requires a healthy dose of that potent word, *trust*. And there are two sides to this coin that need to be addressed.

First, as we have already set out, today's manager is going to have to function in this paradigm of freedom and cooperation. She is required to let go of some of the items that she may hold dear (such as those individual tasks that she knows herself supremely capable of accomplishing), while clinging to the notion that others are to be developed, encouraged and released to accomplish these tasks under their own inspiration. She is to become a motivator, encourager, sometimes enforcer, and grandmaster of the big picture. It is an attitude of mind and heart that for many able people is a challenge to muster!

On the other side of that coin is the responsibility of the manager to help locate and install people with the desire and ability to carry that freedom carefully. It is what *Good to Great* author, Jim Collins, calls *getting the right people on the bus*. While we will not address it at great lengths here, it bears a mention that many executives and managers have seen the hiring process as "finding people to fit the slot," while the wiser executives have seen that having the right people, capable, creative and hungry to succeed, will help any corporate effort to move forward. It means building systems, processes and procedures around the people you employ, as opposed to hiring people to fit those which the company has already developed. This level of trust building and of creating the environment in which it can function is a fundamental for the manager of today.

If your portfolio as a manager includes the processes of hiring individuals, it is imperative that you find good people. Next, you must have in place the plans necessary to provide them with the tools and training that will allow them to complete their tasks creatively and effectively. Then, you will create an atmosphere of trust and responsibility that allows workers to collaborate in the vision of the organization. And yes, you will manage conflicts and problems that arise, as they invariably do. But you will have the right people, working in the right conditions, to deal with them appropriately, and with positive effect.

YOU MAY:

Dictate the expectations and then govern the workers in the process

OR

Train for expectations and then release workers into the process

---

This freedom and trust among coworkers will help to formulate an environment of responsibility. The key to the process will be the manager who sees her job as the development and protection of that environment, and as training workers to make good decisions, rather than dictating all that should be done.

In much of management training, you will find variations of the description and definition of a manager. More or less, however, it will revolve around certain elements. I will call them *planning, organizing, implementing and governing or overseeing.* The additional element of *leadership* should be included as a part of each of these. Basically, these elements of management will not change. The question is actually less about *what* today's manager does than it is about *how* he does it. What are the focal characteristics that allow the manager to plan, organize, implement and govern effectively in today's workplace, within today's corporate culture?

To answer this, I want to provide you with four essential S's of the modern manager's task. The list includes attempts to **strengthen, supply, support and speak**.

Strengthen

Effectiveness in the workplace for the manager today comes at quite the price. The manager must be many things, called upon to perform varieties of functions, and constantly developing strengths and minimizing weaknesses. He must have organizational skills, people skills, technological understanding and good leadership qualities. But in all these things, one of his primary skills, undoubtedly, must be the simple ability to make those working with him better at what they do. He must be a source of inspiration and a builder of expectation in the office.

Michael Jordon was, in my opinion, the best basketball player of his time, and perhaps of any time. (Which admittedly makes me less than original.) His skills were sharp. His athleticism was unquestioned. His commitment to the hard work of becoming a world class athlete was heralded by all. But in interview after interview, when asked what separated Jordon from the rest, his teammates and coaches invariably had an answer ready: it was his ability to make his teammates better. Players were inspired by his play and by his leadership. They wanted to see their own games rise to the level of their premier teammate. They wanted to be like Mike! The team excelled because of the impact of a strengthening leader, ultimately winning six world championships under that influence.

This is the crux of the matter. One person said that the so-called leader with no followers is not leading; he is just out for a walk. The greatest organizational skills and most studied habits of highly effective people will not translate into much if the ability to inspire and strengthen is not accompanying them. The impartation of inspiration for the corporate ends and excitement over individual participation attaining those ends is an essential element of managerial success in today's marketplace.

Supply

Each person working with and under your supervision has abilities with which they can both personally excel and with them, move the team toward its destination as a whole. Finding those skills and utilizing them to the advantage of the whole is a hallmark of good managerial leadership.

The supervisor who spends all of her time checking and rechecking employee behavior, questioning every decision, advising every choice of the workday, is one who will quickly burn out; and more, burn out the workers around her. Governance, as we have defined one of the managerial tasks, should not be defined by the close-eye conduct of many managers. Such a stranglehold will eventually kill the desire and creativity of those working under such leadership.

The good manager will provide training that meets with the vision that he or she is there to inspire. The goals of the organization, or department, which she serves will be set and communicated. The values that drive the corporate vision will be discerned and established. But policing ends and values is not in itself a worthwhile task. Better to train and incorporate them into the mindset and work experience of employees, and then release them to operate freely within the boundaries of that knowledge.

Supplying the appropriate knowledge and practical tools necessary for completing each individual part—getting the training, resources and supplies to the greatest extent possible—is mandatory. Once resourced, employees working in a free and trustworthy environment will, more often than not, surprise you in their ability to move the organization forward toward meeting its ends.

What is the alternative? Loss. It is the potential loss of momentum, loss of creativity and, often, loss of concern on the part of workers. Staff members that are uninterested in the outcomes of the organization, disinterested in the part that they play and simply waiting for a paycheck are not going to bring about great development and achievement. The offerings of ideas and conduct that each one *may* have been able to contribute will be lost in the mix, and the organization will suffer that loss as well.

Having competent, able and inspired people "on the bus", supplied with what they need to do the energized job that they were brought on to do, will bring exceptional progress.

Support

This characteristic of support leans and builds upon the previous two. Once a manager has honed his skills as an inspirational team leader and begun to strengthen the team working with him, and once he has conspired to get the tools and resources necessary into the hands of his coworkers to do their job effectively, he will now turn his attention to the issue of governance.

Once upon a time, in the not-so-distant past, governance in the workplace meant operating as the office sheriff. Making sure the "laws" were followed—that is, the processes and procedures of the office—and enforcing discipline upon the law-breakers constituted the job description. Today, however, management is defined less by such police action, and more by the counseling and mentoring activities that better fit the modern work environment.

The openness and freedom that we defined earlier in this chapter is a central key to this activity. It is, in fact, and indispensable component. Workers must feel supported, and thereby heard and protected when they raise issues. They must understand that they are affirmed and feel encouraged when they produce good results.

Regardless of where a person is positioned on the office food chain, trustful interactivity must replace the territorialism and competition that has been the hallmark of many business environments in days past.

Speak

We have all been to the courses, seminars and training events that have trumpeted one after the other that communication is the main ingredient to all good relationships. This is no less true in the market place than in other areas of life. The flow of information is what builds the trust that we have already expressed is so important for today's management situations. Quite frankly, the more and better things are communicated, the greater the chances of success.

> People in organizations typically spend over 75% of their time in an interpersonal situation; thus it is no surprise to find that at the root of a large number of organizational problems is poor communications. Effective communication is an essential component of organizational success whether it is at the interpersonal, intergroup, intragroup, organizational, or external levels.
>
> -- http://web.cba.neu.edu

Beware, however, that the alternative is just as true. Lack of communication is like clogs in the artery: the oxygen of information is not allowed to get to where it needs to be and suffocation begins.

A few items of concern in this vital area of communication, a discipline so vital to the role of the manager, are worth mentioning here.

First, it must be recognized that the workplace has more means and methods of communication now than ever before, and they work very quickly. Email, intranet systems, message boards and messenger systems, mobile phones and sms; it has all conspired to ensure that word travels fast, whether good or bad. The manager that can not keep the pace is truly in danger of being left behind. Employees will get ahead of the management team, and the flow of information will proceed uncontrolled or ill defined.

Expectations must be communicated clearly and frequently. Changes must be heralded and explained. Affirmations must be sounded out and adequately dispersed throughout the office. Information is the power of today's society, and employees need to feel informed. It is an expression of appreciation for their contributions when they are perceived as being "being kept in the loop". There is no shortage of means for accomplishing this end, and the manager will be tried and judged by the ability and inclination to efficiently communicate with his employees, his peers and his bosses.

There are still some old-world companies out there looking to hire functionaries, or organizations looking to be led by the strong, iron-fisted executive. But by and large, those days are gone, and the task of the competent will be to learn the arts described here: motivation, service, collaboration, freedom, trust, teamwork, in addition to the traditional concerns of professional management. There will be many potential packages that come along—new techniques, development programs, quality management systems, training programs—that will promise the next great leap in the management of a division or a company. In the end, however, it will be those capable of this relational, cooperative leadership that will be recognized as accomplished managers.

The following chart may help provide some food for thought, as you consider your place in today's field of management. The left column illustrates the traditionally held concepts of management, while the right flows with more modern trends in the discipline. Consider these comparisons.

Old Thought Management vs. Managing for Today

Quality: Empowerment

Punishment	Reward
Demands "respect"	Invites speaking out
Drill sergeant	Motivator
Limits and defines	Empowers
Imposes discipline	Values creativity
"Here's what we are going to do!"	"How can I serve you?"
Bottom line	Vision

Quality: Restructure

Control	Change
Rank	Connection
Hierarchy	Network

Rigid	Flexible
Automatic annual raises	Pay for performance
Performance review	Mutual contract for results
Mechanistic	Holistic
Compartmental	Systemic

Quality: Teaching

Order-giving	Facilitating
Military archetype	Teaching archetype

Quality: Role Model

Issues orders	Acts as role model
Demands unquestioning obedience	Coaches and mentors others

Quality: Openness

Keeping people on their toes	Nourishing environment for growth
Reach up/down	Reach out
Information control	Information availability

Quality: Questions and Answers

Knows all the answers	Asks the right questions
Not interested in new answers	Seeks to learn and draw out new ideas

Adapted from *Megatrends for Women.* Patricia Aburdene & John Naisbitt. Villard Books. New York. 1992.

Chapter 2
Managing Work

"Work smarter, not harder." Someone communicated these words to me several years ago, and it forever changed my approach to so many aspects of life. The fact is, work can be a forever expanding affair, and the more innovative one becomes, the more that becomes likely. Without a balanced and careful approach, it can become overwhelming. In this chapter, we will look into some of the basics of managing the workload, including the importance of goal-setting, the governance process associated with achieving goals, and some of the tools necessary for the good manager to keep up with the pace.

SET THE GOALS

> The reason most people never reach their goals is that they don't define them, or ever seriously consider them as believable or achievable. Winners can tell you where they are going, what they plan to do along the way, and who will be sharing the adventure with them.
>
> - Denis Watley
>
> Goals are dreams with deadlines.
>
> - Diana Scharf Hunt
>
> Quoted on www.goal-setting-guide.com

We begin with what may be considered one of the most central functions of any good management leader: *the setting of goals.* In the normal sense, the overall purpose of a company or organization is set by its top leadership. We often refer to this as the vision of the company. Then, each level of management is responsible for developing plans for the completion of their segment of the goals associated with that vision, and the processes for seeing it through to completion. Managers and workers must work in unison to develop these goals, and to complete them in a timely fashion.

The purpose of goal-setting, obviously, is to help formulate a road map for paths ahead that you and the team plan to travel. A good plan will include the elements necessary for achieving the goal(s), as well as time schedules for reaching each step as the journey unfolds. Without the purposeful setting of destination in this manner, work tends to go along fleetingly, individual accomplishments do not build into the greater good, and ultimately little work of lasting value is performed.

Goals, however, must be developed intelligently. Setting goals for the sake of having them will prove as ineffective as having none stated at all. Choosing the appropriate goals, prioritizing them, and developing them in a useful, understandable and achievable fashion are of utmost importance!

Well planned, thoughtful goals produce much fruit for the efforts of management. Firstly, they provide direction for each individual and the group as a whole that lead toward the achieving of particular ends. While I can not, unfortunately, attribute this quote to its original source, I still find that it contains too much wisdom to withhold it. Perhaps you have heard it as well. "If you don't know where you are going, you are sure to get there!"

Not many organizations are content with having divisions or departments wandering aimlessly through their appointed tasks. For sure, with competent people on board, it may be that something of value will actually be produced. But will that product be meaningful? Will it contribute to the value of the overall effort of the company? Will it advance the vision that has been set forward by the senior management? Without a plan, *something* can be done. But it may not be the *right thing.*

It is an age-old proverb that rings with proven truth: without a vision (guiding principles), people cast off restraint. They wander about just doing things; without combining those things into a coherent and useful whole. Ultimately, the effort finishes or fizzles out at a point of incompleteness.

Goals are targets with a timeframe. They provide attainable steps toward getting you to where you want to go. Without them, you will be given to the unfortunate results of wasted time and wasted effort. You will find yourself working harder, rather than smarter.

Secondly, goals will help you to achieve by providing standards of measurement. As particular goals are achieved, or at least steps within the process are completed, you can visualize how far you have come and how far is left to go. A larger goal may be divided into smaller, more immediate segments, allowing for the constant forward movement that is necessary to achieving the end.

We all like to feel that something is happening. Few things will break down morale and generate work fatigue as quickly as the feeling that, "We're just doing the same old things over and over again. We're going nowhere." But when goals are achieved, one by one and step by step, the feeling of accomplishment helps to propel the effort forward.

Thirdly, goals help people to understand the part that their individual efforts contribute to the ultimate ends. If goals are not created and communicated, then you will find workers drifting in their tasks, perhaps duplicating efforts (or, worse yet, competing over the same efforts) and picking and choosing their way through the myriad of tasks that need to be finalized. Clarity is always a positive force in getting individuals to comply with and contribute to a greater plan. As each one knows what he or she is to be working toward, and sees how that part fits into the greater whole, the sense of purpose that it generates may be expected to increase effort and deliver positive results.

Finally, goals can be positive motivators. When it is clear that each effort is contributing to something greater than the simple, mundane tasks that meet the employee day by day, the greater the chance of enjoying—or at least positively enduring—those tasks. Beyond that, setting goals that push workers beyond their usual level of performance, and stretching them toward grander accomplishments can help to break the routine and instill a new sense of purpose. Employees may not need to enjoy every task that they are required to perform, but if they can find some joy in seeing the bigger picture, and be granted the opportunity to contribute to that greater picture in ever increasing ways, the more that commitment and passion will be applied to the workload.

In his book *Good to Great*, Jim Collins identifies a unique approach to vision and goals on the part of the world's greatest companies. Each of them has committed to setting their sights on being the best at what they do. The vision is singular, and the goals associated with that vision are all purposeful in pressing toward that unified objective. Getting everyone to work together toward that point of excellence and accomplishment is a fundamental pursuit of the good manager. It has been said that the best goals are:

- Not too plentiful.
- Simple and specific.
- Relatively difficult, so that they inspire, but
- Easy enough to ensure accomplishment, and
- Are based on team work and participation.

If this is true, then what is the method for creating and implementing good goals? We have all been in those meetings where discussion is generated, plans are floated, needs and desires are outlined, and then, much to the dismay of everyone involved, the follow through is neglected. It is time wasted and effort lost. Just another think-tank session that did more tanking than thinking. The result of this kind of effort (or lack of it) is a cycle of activity that leaves teams feeling immobilized. Work feels superfluous, and morale declines. Motivation, in these instances, is effectively killed. So the wise leader knows that the path must be paved toward purpose!

More than a few books, courses and seminars have utilized what is known as the SMART method of goal setting. I find this to be useful as well, so rather than re-create the wheel, I will join them in the use of this approach.

SMART Goal Setting

SMART goal setting begins by taking a look at each potential goal and evaluating it, making any changes necessary to ensure it meets the following criteria for a SMART goal:

S = Specific
M = Measurable
A = Attainable
R = Realistic
T = Timely

Specific

Goals should be as clearly expressed and as concise as possible, emphasizing what should be its specific result. For example, the sales goal of a region might be "to increase sales this quarter by 20 percent," as opposed to, "to significantly increase the number of sales this quarter." Being specific helps to focus the collective effort and channel the best contributions that individuals have to offer. *Specific goals should reveal exactly what is expected of personnel, in what time frame, why it is important, and what resources should be utilized to accomplish the goal.*

Measurable

The goal that can not be measured can not be meaningfully managed. If you can not tell where in the sequence of events employees stand at any given time, then you can not gauge the distance remaining until completion of the goal. Interim measurements (step by step segments or portions) are quite helpful in this regard. These we call *objectives*.

An example is often given of the woman desiring to lose weight. It is a poor plan to begin with "I purpose to lose weight," whereas the goal, "I shall lose ten pounds in three weeks," is both specific and measurable.

When you set such goals in your projects, you instill the potential to assess progress and keep the project moving forward cohesively, on time and with the momentum that comes with a sense of progress.

Attainable

Flowing from the idea of having measurable goals is the task of setting attainable goals. Remember, goals are dreams with a deadline. The fulfillment of the dream will depend upon meeting the deadline—or, the segmented deadlines along the way. In this way, you move toward developing the attitudes of expectation and accomplishment that are necessary to ultimately reach your destination.

Goals that are set too far "out there"; that is, they are nearly impossible to reach, will almost certainly result in failure, and the sense of defeat which accompanies it. We have stated before that it is essential to set big goals in order to be challenged, stretched and launched toward achievement. But you can easily defeat your task if the goals are beyond the realm of realistic.

This is another reason that it is important to break your ultimate goal (the big dream) into smaller, more do-able segments. These smaller goals that you set—that is, segments of the greater goal—should be large enough to challenge and inspire, but realistic enough to accomplish with a committed effort. This will keep the process moving along, with the sense of purpose and accomplishment that is necessary for positive morale.

Realistic

The setting of **specific, measurable, attainable** goals should not be confused with the ideas of simple or small. It can be tempting to use these guidelines to dumb down the process of planning. We have made it clear, however, that goals must be grand enough to stretch and inspire. Such planning mandates commitment among workers, and challenges them enough to see good work done, both in terms of quantity and quality.

Realistic goal setting is done by looking inward to see what tools are in place in regards to people and resources, and then organizing them into projects that lean on those strengths and stretch them just enough to challenge performance. The goal, however, can not be set outside the boundaries of what can actually be accomplished with the resources that are available. Stretch them; don't tear them apart. Setting goals too low will fail to inspire, if not actually kill inspiration, whereas setting them too high will create panic and a sense of impending failure. If you plan for workers to succeed by setting goals at the outer edges of their abilities while remaining safely within reasonable boundaries, then you will lay the groundwork for achievement.

Timely

"Don't do today what you can put off again tomorrow." I read this on a refrigerator magnet one time. And oh how true it can be. Those of use prone to procrastination are often victims to the fact that we will delay tasks, especially unpleasant tasks, again and again, for as long as we are even remotely able. And as a manager, you can assume that the majority of your work force is numbered among us.

Goals that are set without defined timetables are simply recipes for procrastination and hyper-deliberation. As much time as is provided will undoubtedly be the amount utilized to complete the task given. Usually, it will require even more! For this reason, you must eliminate the potential by setting clear, reasonable time limits for each goal or objective.

Simply put, "SMART" goals will make for smart work. Smart work yields smart results. Too often, however, you will find that goals are set poorly, without clarity, lacking the specific, measurable, attainable, realistic and timely characteristics of goals that are built to succeed!

You will find that as you work through this simple list, your own processes for planning will become more focused and sensible. (That is, if you have not already been functioning in such an organized manner.) You will be implementing what the website Time-Management-Guide.com identifies as the differences between **goals** and **objectives**. Pay attention, because this distinction is important to you.

Objectives are indeed goals, but they are the smaller parts of the whole: the segments designed in reasonable and achievable forms. Some important questions for you to answer when you are deliberating the breaking down of goals into objectives include:

- What conditions are necessary for this to be performed and completed?
- What resources—material, people and otherwise—are required?
- What skills and knowledge need to be developed?
- Is there anything else necessary to be achieved first?
- When does this need to be done?

You can formulate the answers to these into specific objectives necessary for reaching the overall goal. "We must complete these items in order to achieve this goal." Your task is to create parts that relate to the whole, segmenting the work into SMART objectives that combine to achieve the larger goal.

The heavens themselves, the planets and this centre observe degree, priority and place." – Shakespeare

It is good to remember also that the **larger goal may be firm and inflexible**, but the objectives to reaching that goal are not. Flexibility and creativity in the approach to difficulties, challenges and changes along the way will help the work flow. If the current manner of achieving an objective is not working, you must consider a new approach. But stick to the goal!

Too many goals!

As you get excited about setting smart, organizational goals, keep in mind that there is such a thing as goal overload! Just as important as having smart goals is the requirement to have a reasonable number of them. Too many board rooms and strategy planning sessions have revealed over the years that establishing too many "do-able" goals actually defeats them and makes them, at least as a whole, "un-do-able." Crowding the agenda with a mass of objectives and goals will simply overcrowd and choke the process. To avoid this danger, simply apply a few rules to your decision-making as it regards goal setting.

- **Prioritize your goals**. Ask: Which are the most essential? Which will contribute most to the larger picture?

- **Timeline your goals**. Ask: Which of these should be accomplished before the others? Which are required for other objectives or goals to be met?

- **Examine your goals**. Ask: Is this goal still relevant to our mission as it stands now? Is this goal working? Is it still SMART?

Value your goals!

Finally, always remember that your goals and organizational values work together. When we say, "Value your goals," we do not mean only to place value on them, but to root them in the values that have been enshrined in your organization. Make sure that the goals that you set do not contradict these values in any way. For example, if **equality** is a stated value of your organization, do not plan goals that cause one group of workers or a particular department to take unfair advantage of another one. Make sure always that *the way that you work sets the example for what you desire to accomplish.* The organization working for "truth and justice" would be ill served by teaching its workers to lie to the press or give preference to special interest groups.

> **First say to yourself what you would be; and then do what you have to do.**
>
> **-- Epictitus**

USE THE GOALS

Once you have worked at setting goals and objectives of your area of responsibility, the question then becomes what to do with those goals? Without putting them into effect, they remain dead ideas on a page in an office someplace. Here are some helpful thoughts for helping you to launch ideas into the realm of practice!

Communicate, communicate, communicate!

There are a number of ways for you to get the word out to your employees and coworkers. There are also some pitfalls to avoid along the way. Let's discuss these.

Firstly, whether it is a group of executives laboring over the grand vision of an organization, or managers hashing over objectives and goals, one of the great dangers is that, by the time the vision or goal is established, those working on it are tired of it. The process of developing goals and strategies can be long work, sometimes intense, sometimes tiring. Therefore, by the time the goal is created, it can feel like the end in itself. A collective breath is let out that, finally, a laborious task has ended, and everyone is just anxious to get back to other concerns.

But that is not the end. It must be communicated. Again and again, and then again, until the point of completion, the purpose must be spoken. In the case of the organizational vision, it must be an endless concern to make it known. It is just as important to communicate the vision and goals to others *with energy and excitement* as it is to do the work of developing them in the first place. You must communicate to workers the importance of that aim, just as it was important for you to labor over its creation. If you can not do this, then you can expect nothing more than dull performance when it comes time to do the work. Uninspired people have little reason to bring in great performances. For the cause of vision, "Do not grow weary in well doing!"

When it comes to communicating goals, there are some important tips to keep in mind:

- Always communicate goals in writing.

- Personalize the communication. One large event to let everyone know what is going on will never be enough. As personal as the communication can be, that is the level that you want to achieve, with each one in the process.

- Groups or teams involved in common goals should also be addressed corporately. Each person's contribution to the group should be publicly outlined and made clear.

- Make it participatory, as much as possible. In other words, get input from groups or individuals regarding the goals assigned to them. As much as their contributions can be incorporated into the goal, they should be.

It can not be overemphasized how important it is to keep communicating the goals, and the related objectives, that are the priorities of your area of oversight. Two of the greatest obstacles to achievement of your goals are the sense of normality that come with the average workday and the sense of the mundane that can accompany daily tasks. Once vision has been cast, and goals have been set, then the initial rush that accompanies new plans and dreams are too soon replaced with these negative sensations.

The good manager will learn to stay personally focused on the set goals, as well as to continue refocusing other people on the same. This can be difficult as the events and interruptions of each day rush into the work place. For this reason, it must be a priority for the manager to refresh herself and her workers in this regard on a constant basis.

Remember that, in the activity of the day, the main thing has to stay the main thing. The temptation can be to get easily side-tracked, or to concentrate on small, more easily completed tasks. (It is only natural to gravitate to the easy items left to be done.) This often leads to higher priorities being left for a time that never seems to arrive. You must focus on the larger aspects, or break the larger into smaller, more do-able parts. But let the main things be the main things.

Also, be committed to personal responsibility for your own agenda. Time management and the organization of your schedule can not be left to any other person. Many people spend enormous amounts of time in the process of determining what they should be doing, as opposed to getting something done. The good manager must have organizational skills that extend beyond the immediate!

Another aspect of this personal responsibility is the controlling of interruptions. They will come. From bosses, from coworkers, from employees and from customers, interruptions will always be a part of the work day. Knowing when to be available and when not to be is essential to good time usage and quality management. Being faithful to cut off the non-essential and turn to the important matters of the day will mark the efforts of any good manager. Using your goals to your advantage includes using them to guide the use of your time, and to limit these interruptions.

GOVERN THE GOALS

Goals will never actually work to the advantage of an organization until they are truly turned into active pursuits. This is an essential characteristic of a quality manager! The fact is that few people will have the opportunity to shape the workday and the activities of employees more than you, as we have stated before. So, what should you be doing with that knowledge? Governing, overseeing, coaching, encouraging and cheer-leading the goals!

This governing process is admittedly delicate. The success of any organization unavoidably rests on the abilities of each person involved, and how those abilities are translated into action.

We outlined in the first chapter some of the positives and negatives of the management process today. Because of the modern work environment, the shape of governance has changed. There is a balance required because too little governance brings chaos, too much breeds stagnation. Still, it rests upon you, the manager, to find that balance, and to see that the vision and goals of the organization are pursued and accomplished, using the appropriate resources, and delivering the end result in a timely fashion. To do this, you must be able to manage your goals, and the people involved in accomplishing them.

What follows are guidelines that the wise manager would do well to heed in order to govern the goals so important to the success of the organization, and therefore to his own career goals! We have touched some of these before, but it bears repeating them in this context.

1. **Governance is not policing**. It is not your primary task to watch for impending mistakes; nor is it to punish them when they are committed. Instead, you support the effort of the workers, seeing that they have what is needed to succeed, and that they are committed to achieving objectives in an allotted time.

Checking in and providing guidance and help are good. Micromanaging through excessive involvement and/or making a requirement of incessant reports will only yield resentment... and duplicate (or triplicate!) efforts.

2. **Monitoring is, however, essential.** You are not the office sheriff, but that does not mean that you can let the workload alone. It is imperative that you stay informed as to the progress and the needs of those working on the organizational goals left to your care. Goals are deliberate. They are not activities left to time and chance.

3. **Units of measurement must be determined and made clear in every given area of the goal.** Your workers need to know how their progress will be reviewed and judged. Each goal or objective must have some kind of quantifiable end in mind— whether a time frame or the delivery of a specific product. Whatever measurement is to be used, it must be relevant to the task at hand, and it must be communicated clearly so that expectations are well understood.

4. **Success and failure in meeting goals or objectives must be communicated.** This is often called the power of feedback. Obviously, positive feedback is the preferred course. Workers respond to the knowledge, and the subsequent appreciation that comes with it, that a job has been well done. There will be times that negative reports must be given, but it is an imperative that as much positive reinforcement as possible be utilized in the feedback

process. Things that can be expressed positively rather than negatively should be.

5. **Corporate and personal issues should be handled separately.** Feedback that relates to the progress of the team working toward a common goal should be communicated to the group as a whole, publicized in common areas, etc. Personal issues, and especially notifications of any shortcomings in the performance of individuals, are better handled in private. Your objective is always to get the unit to work together toward common success. With each individual, it is to get the best possible performance from that individual to meet the corporate goal.

6. **Monitoring of performance should be *systematic*.** These last items lead us to the issue of the monitoring and evaluating of performance on both the corporate and individual levels. This process must take place in order for goals to be effectively governed. Some thoughts to take into account include:

   • Assignments, projects and personnel should be monitored continually. (But remember: governed, not policed!) This process means consistently measuring performance and providing feedback to employees and work groups on their progress toward reaching the goals.

   • Because the requirements for monitoring of performance include conducting progress reviews with employees, the ongoing process provides the opportunity to check into how well they are meeting the set goals. *It also allows the manager and the organization to make changes to unrealistic expectations or problematic standards for performance.*

- By the process of monitoring continually, unacceptable performance can be identified at any time during the review period and assistance may be provided to address such issues. This is much better than the alternative, which is to wait until the end of the period when summary rating levels are assigned.

Key Performance Indicators (KPI's)

There are three areas of activity within an organization that are critical to commercial and professional success, and therefore KPIs need to be established in each:

1) Measurements relating to financial performance and business development;
2) Views of clients about the range, provision and delivery of the organization's services;
3) Views of personnel about all aspects of their relationship with the organization.

A successful professional firm will typically start by identifying and agreeing specific KPIs and considering how best to measure them.

---

7. **A systematic monitoring process must be more than an idea**. It must be actualized. This is the real concern of a good manager, and the fact is that there are many paths that can lead to the same destination. In the end, however, it is up to management to implement the best monitoring

practices for their own organization, department or project. The task is simple: find a way to enact governance effectively in your environment. A suggestion, however, follows.

In the book *Good to Great*, Jim Collins identified the fact that many employees lack a sense of fulfillment in their jobs. This he portrays as a large detriment to many companies, holding them back from excellence in their market places. While many, if not most, performance monitoring systems tend to center on such items as quantifiable productivity reports, these numbers can not always reveal what is truly taking place within the company. At the end of the day, it is the employees that must make the difference in the company.

For this reason, we suggest that monitoring based upon employee satisfaction and contribution can help the organization to excel, beyond that of the results of number crunching.

- Settle the values and subsequent conduct that is the desired product of each employee. (Examples may be job attendance and punctuality, introduction of creative solutions, safety on the job, etc.)

- Enshrine that conduct in a standardized process of measurement. (An example may be a system of points assigned to particular kinds of conduct that are awarded for compliance and taken away for violations.)

- Have regular times designed to reward employees with affirmation and applause when that conduct is performed to a degree of excellence. Creation of something public and visible as a reward will help to inspire the pursuit of that conduct. (As opposed to the negative rebuke that often publicly takes place in the work place.)

Creating a way for workers to feel participatory, appreciated and fulfilled in their work environment is a key to performance.

Measure the progress!

Obviously, the goal of all of this process of governance is simply to see how you and your coworkers are proceeding toward the completion of your goals. We have been working through some of the issues of that monitoring process, but now we need to put a little more meat to the skeleton in order to help today's manager find effective ways of implementing these ideals.

We will submit to you that you can plan your progress as a team by creating **MAPS** for your goals: **markers, activities, priorities and schedules**.

1. **Markers**: Determine and chart periods of time or units of measurement, markers, that allow you to visualize how far you have come within any given objective or goal, and how far is left to go. When you have passed each marker, you may highlight that fact, even celebrate it together, and then urge progress toward the next marker.

2. **Activities:** Outline the duties of each person or team in achieving every objective or marker. These

may be monitored to see how far they have come, what needs to be accomplished next, and how far it is to the next marker of achievement.

3. **Priorities**: Some activities must be completed before others in order to achieve each marker in the process of goal accomplishment. Prioritizing the activities, without creating stifled or stagnant progress, can be a balancing act. You do not want to create log jams in the work activity, with certain workers waiting on the work of others before they can or will act. People should be free, as much as possible, to proceed with their assignments and maintain solid momentum. It is useful, however, to have an idea of the best flow of progress, item by item.

4. **Schedules**: Realistically setting timeframes for each activity or marker is an art. It requires knowledge of your employees and their abilities. It also requires a sense of timing for each of these various parts. The task of setting schedules for accomplishing goals is often one of the more difficult aspects of project planning, as they must be strict enough to ensure a proper work pace, while still allowing enough flexibility for realism. It must account as well for the inevitable, unexpected challenges that will arise. Good time planning will be one of the greatest servants to assist in reaching your markers, and ultimately accomplishing your goals.

Some useful tools for managing the "mapping" process are included as appendixes to this chapter. Well known methods like the use of Gantt-style bar charts and other flowcharts are excellent contributors to the effective development of quality work.

These applications are sure to assist you in the process of monitoring progress.

> **It is important, and quite relieving, to know that there are wonderful software products now available to help you in the course of your planning. As it pertains to the bar and flowcharts described in the addendum, Microsoft Project® and Milestones® are two premier products that you should take into account!**

Praise successes and highlight challenges!

Communication is always the oil in the machinery of a performing organization. It is imperative throughout the processes of both goal planning and monitoring to ensure that communication is always taking place, at the beginning, middle and end. Once goals have been set, progress has been managed, and output has been completed, it is important to examine the results with your coworkers. Critical examination adds essential value to the work processes. First, look together at the stated goals and objectives (markers). Were they achieved as planned? By the assigned people? Using the appropriate resources? And on time?

Now, analyze these results. Take special notice of those who met or outperformed expectations. Go over the results of individual performance with each worker, and together as a group examine the overall effectiveness of the work that was done. Choose a good, appropriate manner for rewarding and/or challenging employees for the work that was done.

Make sure that work does not finish, and that goals do not drift by, without properly communicating the end results.

Addendum to Chapter 2
Bar Charts and Flow Charts

1. GANTT-STYLE BAR CHARTS

This is one of the best known and most utilized methods of tracking progress. Henry Laurence Gantt (1861-1919) was a mechanical engineer, management consultant and industry advisor. He developed Gantt charts in the second decade of the 20th century. Gantt charts were used as a visual tool to show scheduled and actual progress of projects. Accepted as a commonplace project management tool today, it was an innovation of world-wide importance in the 1920s. Gantt charts were used on large construction projects like the Hoover Dam started in 1931 and the interstate highway network started in 1956.

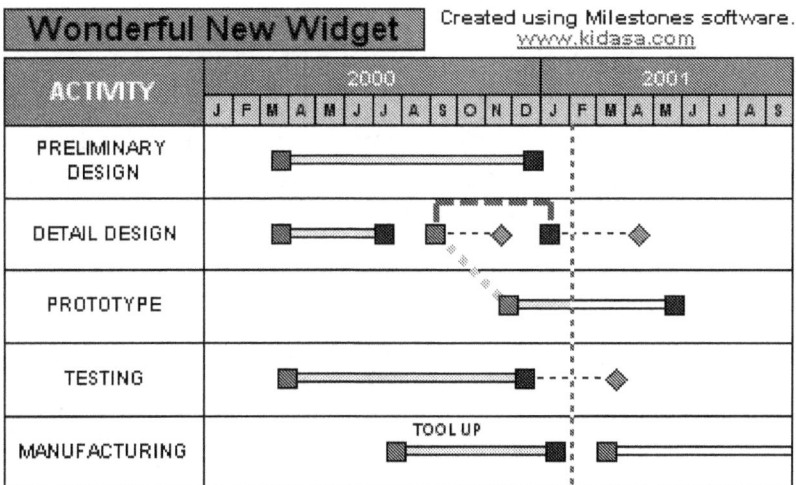

Wonderful New Widget	Created using Milestones software. www.kidasa.com																		
ACTIVITY	2000												2001						
	J	F	M	A	M	J	J	A	S	O	N	D	J	F	M	A	M	J	J	A	S
PRELIMINARY DESIGN																					
DETAIL DESIGN																					
PROTOTYPE																					
TESTING																					
MANUFACTURING							TOOL UP														

A Gantt chart is

- A useful tool for the processes of planning and scheduling projects.
- A graphical representation of the duration of tasks against the progression of time.
- Helpful when monitoring a project's progress.

Planning and Scheduling

- A Gantt chart allows you to assess how long a project should take.
- It lays out the order in which tasks need to be carried out.
- It helps manage the dependencies between tasks.

Monitoring A Project

- A Gantt chart allows you to see immediately what should have been achieved at a point in time.
- It allows you to see how remedial action may bring the project back on course.

A Gantt chart is a matrix.

- The Gantt chart is constructed with a horizontal axis representing the total time span of the project, broken down into increments (days, weeks, or months).
- It is constructed with a vertical axis representing the tasks that make up the project.
- It is constructed with a graph area which contains horizontal bars for each task connecting the period start and period ending symbols.

The Gantt chart has variants.

- Milestones (what we have termed "markers"): important checkpoints or interim goals for a project.
- Resources ("activities"): for team projects, it often helps to have an additional column containing numbers or initials which identify who on the team is responsible for the task.
- Dependencies ("priorities"): an essential concept that some activities are dependent on other activities being completed first.
- Status ("schedules"): the projects progress, the chart is updated by filling in the task's bar to a length proportional to the amount of work that has been finished.

All information above has been obtained from www.ganttchart.com.

2. FLOW CHARTS

Introduction to Flow Charts

The flowchart is a means of visually presenting the flow of data through an information processing systems, the operations performed within the system and the sequence in which they are performed. What follows is an outline of a program flowchart, which describes what operations (and in what sequence) are required to solve a given problem. The program flowchart can be likened to the blueprint of a building. As we know a designer draws a blueprint before starting construction on a building. Similarly, a programmer prefers to draw a flowchart prior to writing a computer program. As in the case of the drawing of a blueprint, the flowchart is drawn according to defined rules and using standard flowchart symbols prescribed by the American National Standard Institute, Inc.

The Meaning of a Flow Chart

A flowchart is a diagrammatic representation that illustrates the sequence of operations to be performed to get the solution of a problem. Flowcharts are generally drawn in the early stages of formulating computer solutions. Flowcharts facilitate communication between programmers and business people. These flowcharts play a vital role in the programming of a problem and are quite helpful in understanding the logic of complicated and lengthy problems. Once the flowchart is drawn, it becomes easy to write the program in any level language. Often we see how flowcharts are helpful in explaining the program to others. Hence, it is correct to say that a flowchart is a must for the better documentation of a complex program.

Guidelines for Drawing a Flow Chart

Flowcharts are usually drawn using some standard symbols; however, some special, personalized symbols can also be developed when required. Some standard symbols, which are frequently required for flowcharting many computer programs, are shown in the figure on the next page.

Flowchart Symbols

The following are some helpful guidelines in the work of flowcharting:

1. In drawing a proper flowchart, all necessary requirements should be listed out in logical order.
2. The flowchart should be clear, neat and easy to follow. There should not be any room for ambiguity in understanding the flowchart.
3. The usual direction of the flow of a procedure or system is from left to right or top to bottom.
4. Only one flow line should come out from a process symbol.

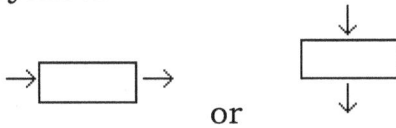

$$\rightarrow\boxed{}\rightarrow \qquad \text{or} \qquad \downarrow\boxed{}\downarrow$$

5. Only one flow line should enter a decision symbol, but two or three flow lines, one for each possible answer, should leave the decision symbol.

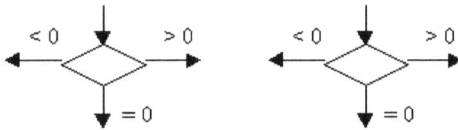

Standard Symbols for Flowcharting

Symbol	Description
(rounded rectangle)	Start or end of the program
(rectangle)	Computational steps or processing function of a program
(parallelogram)	Input or output operation
(diamond)	Decision making and branching
(circle)	Connector or joining of two parts of program

(magnetic tape symbol)	Magnetic Tape
(magnetic disk symbol)	Magnetic Disk
(off-page connector symbol)	Off-page connector
← → ↑ ↓	Flow line
----[	Annotation
(display symbol)	Display

6. Only one flow line is used in conjunction with terminal symbol.

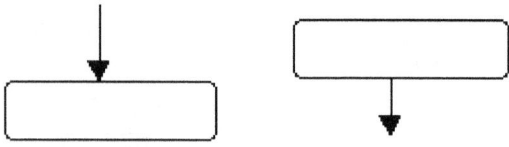

7. Write within standard symbols briefly. As necessary, you can use the annotation symbol to describe data or computational steps more clearly.

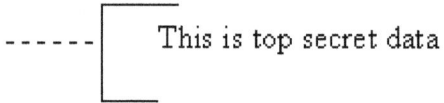

```
------[  This is top secret data
```

8. If the flowchart becomes complex, it is better to use connector symbols to reduce the number of flow

lines. Avoid the intersection of flow lines if you want to make it more effective and better way of communication.

9. Ensure that the flowchart has a logical *start* and *finish.*
10. It is useful to test the validity of the flowchart by passing through it with a simple test data.

Advantages of Flow Charts

1. Communication: Flowcharts are better way of communicating the logic of a system to all concerned.
2. Effective analysis: With the help of flowchart, problem can be analyzed in more effective way.
3. Proper documentation: Program flowcharts serve as a good program documentation, which is needed for various purposes.
4. Efficient Coding: The flowcharts act as a guide or blueprint during the systems analysis and program development phase.
5. Proper Debugging: The flowchart helps in debugging process.
6. Efficient Program Maintenance: The maintenance of operating program becomes easy with the help of flowchart. It helps the programmer to put efforts more efficiently on that part

LIMITATIONS OF USING FLOWCHARTS

1. Complex logic: Sometimes, the program logic is quite complicated. In that case, flowchart becomes complex and clumsy.
2. Alterations and Modifications: If alterations are required the flowchart may require re-drawing completely.

3. Reproduction: As the flowchart symbols cannot be typed, reproduction of flowchart becomes a problem.
4. The essentials of what is done can easily be lost in the technical details of how it is done.

Example: Flow Chart

Find the largest of three numbers A, B, and C.

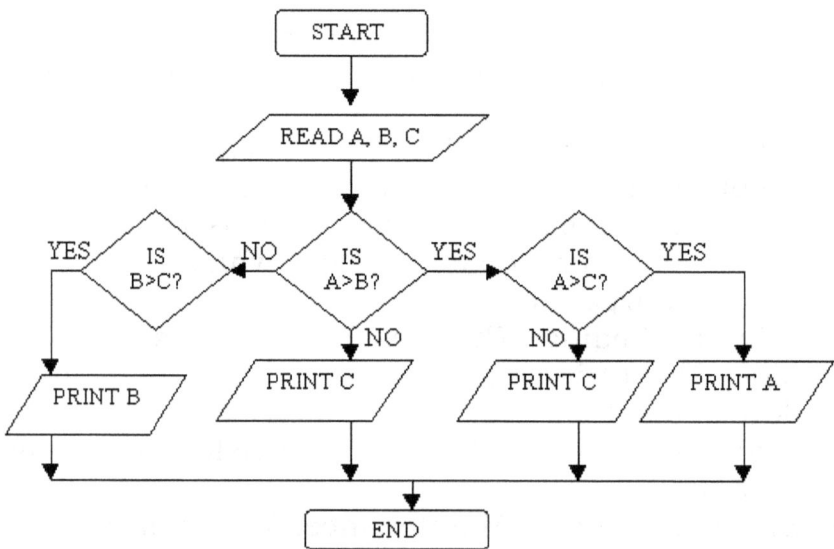

```
                    ┌──────────┐
                    │  START   │
                    └──────────┘
                         │
                         ▼
                  ╱ READ A, B, C ╱
                         │
                         ▼
YES  ◇ IS        NO    ◇ IS      YES   ◇ IS       YES
     B>C?   ◄──────    A>B?   ──────►  A>C?
   ◇                 ◇                ◇
   │                   │NO             NO│           │
   ▼                   ▼                 ▼            ▼
╱ PRINT B ╱      ╱ PRINT C ╱      ╱ PRINT C ╱   ╱ PRINT A ╱
   │                   │                 │            │
   ▼                   ▼                 ▼            ▼
                    ┌──────────┐
                    │   END    │
                    └──────────┘
```

All information above is obtained from www.nos.org.

Chapter 3
Managing People

In the same manner that it is important to set and monitor goals, it is very necessary to the life of an organization to ensure that the people associated with the work are coached, monitored, and evaluated. This should be done for review of job performance, certainly, but also for the good of individual development, which is a benefit to the work place and all coworkers. *It is the task of every good manager to oversee not only the work, but also the people under his or her care.*

INDIVIDUAL PERFORMANCE EVALUATIONS

It has been posited in some circles that the task of individual performance evaluation is just as likely to be a detrimental one as an affirming or constructive one. That point has some validity, if in fact evaluations are not handled well. The avoidance of evaluation, however, can be detrimental to the work that is performed, and to the atmosphere in which it all takes place.

It is a dreaded task to take on the responsibility of evaluating workers. Indeed, it is probably one of the most avoided, if possible, and certainly one of the least pursued among managers. This situation could be challenged and overturned, however, if the task was submitted to some guidelines that can help to ensure a profitable, if not enjoyable, time for both manager and employee. It is always to the benefit of the worker, the manager and the organization when performance evaluation is taken seriously and done well. Consider the following pointers.

1. **Mangers and workers must see the task as a constructive and affirmative one.**

The process of performance evaluations which takes place between the manager and the worker can be one of beneficial use of time and opportunistic communication. If the manager is attuned to the fact that most employees do, in fact, want to be aware of their level of performance, but that they want the communication to be constructive rather than just corrective, then she may use that attitude to her advantage.

Consider that communication between manager and employee—the personal, one-on-one kind—is often limited by time and opportunity in the course of average workdays. Performance evaluations offer a set time and a systematic approach that allows for there to be quality communication. Expectations, priorities and the perceptions of productivity often differ quite dramatically between the manager and those who are the "managed." This is a time to get together, and attempt to get on the same page.

What might flow out from that personal communication could be a beneficial learning process. Managers might learn more about the individual worker, his or her desire for advancement, any job satisfaction issues that exist, and/or other development concerns that often have little or no time to be communicated. The opportunity to outline and share with the worker what is necessary for his or her career advancement is an indispensable part of encouragement into more responsibility, and helpful in providing the framework for such advance to occur. Such communication benefits both sides of the management equation with constructive analysis.

Finally, performance evaluations allow for there to be documentation of the worker's progress. When it comes to issues of career development, promotion potential, or dismissal, when necessary, it is *imperative* to have these records in place and thereby have the ability to show the employee and others (executives, lawyers, judges, etc.) the reason for a manager's choice of dealings with that person.

Performance evaluations can be a pleasant and constructive element in the work dynamic between manager and employee, between the employee and the company, and in his or her contribution to the work environment. It need not be dreadful or unproductive.

2. **The process of performance evaluation does not need to be overly intense or difficult**. There is a way to simplify the task.

One of the reasons that managers would often choose to avoid performance evaluations, if allowed to do so, is because they are often very task-oriented, and such dealings with *people* are often viewed as distractions to their preferred or more highly prioritized *activities*.

What can result is a process whereby the evaluations are brushed off and not completed purposefully, or done in such a loose way as to get everyone appeased and moving along in their workloads. Whether it is by an overly intense agenda, or a fluffy and therefore useless one, performance evaluations can be relegated to the pile of the useless unless the manager and employee come to a cooperative place.

This can be helped by understanding that the process does not have to be so cumbersome or intimidating. In fact, a simple approach to performance evaluations can help both the evaluator and the evaluated to gain positive results from the procedure.

Although a performance evaluation usually ends with a formal report of some nature that is standardized for each organization, it is worthwhile to remember that evaluation does not begin only at the time of a planned, specific event. *It begins with the beginning of an objective, and carries throughout the entire timeframe coming under evaluation!* Managers must be attentive to progress and performance throughout the duration of a project, not only at the formal, evaluation time.

With the use of the formal evaluation, however, there are a few helpful items to keep in mind that will make managerial efforts valuable.

- A copy of the written evaluation should be given to the employee for review, complete with any feedback that the manger feels pertinent to the evaluation. Examples of positive and negative behavior should be included, and any available documentation attached. If the manager has the luxury of formatting the evaluation report, it should be kept as simple as possible, while still completing its purpose fully.

- Do not just provide the written evaluation and run. Cover the items in the report face-to-face, stressing positives and encouraging the potential for development in any shortcomings that are evident. Avoid confrontational situations, unless absolutely necessary; rather, frame and communicate things in positive statements.

- Use the evaluation process to set new goals, both in terms of work progress as well as in areas of personal development and career advancement.

3. **A little preparation for the evaluation process can go a long way to making the time spent more purposeful and less cumbersome.**

It is important to allow workers time to be prepared for what is expected of their evaluation, as will be further described below. It is equally important, however, that the diligent manager is also prepared.

Give credibility to the evaluation process by not making it a last minute affair. Know what you are expecting to review with the worker. Spend adequate time in reviewing the worker's file from throughout the evaluation period to be able to speak intelligently and freshly about his or her performance.

Performance evaluations treated lightly by the manager will not command much greater faith or credence from the employee. The manager is required to set the bar.

4. **Communication is the key to success, always.**

The weight that is applied to evaluations in terms of salary and career advancement obviously puts a lot of pressure on the evaluation process. Both the employee and the manager are usually quite aware of the stakes. This pressure adds to the complexity of having to address perceived strengths and weaknesses and subsequent advancement (or lack of it). As a package, it could be quite over-whelming.

But what allows much of the pressure to be alleviated is that the evaluation process needs not be, and should not be, a one-time or few-times-per-year process. Just as the evaluation itself is a beginning to end affair, so is the communication that results in evaluation. The good manager will make it about the interaction that takes place throughout the period of evaluation—clearly stated values, goals, objectives and timeframes—and will not rely solely upon the short event that takes place at formal evaluation time. It is rather like the teaching methodology instructor that once encouraged me, "if you want your students to do well on the test, make sure they know what is expected from the testing." Just as school exams should not be about trick questions and obscure answers, performance evaluations should not be about "dropping a bomb" on the employee at evaluation. If he or she knows what to expect throughout, and knows what criteria will be utilized in judgment, then performance evaluations can simply be reinforcement of already shared knowledge and expectations.

When it comes time to formally write and state evaluation summaries, there are some helpful items to assist you in that evaluation.

- Do not outline failures and shortcomings only. A point by point breakdown of negative outcomes, unaccompanied by any recognition of the things done well will only serve to alienate and repress most people. A little encouragement can go a long way.

- Do not criticize, and especially do not highlight inadequate results of expectations that you, the manager, failed to communicate clearly. If a job was left to be done poorly throughout the period without ever being addressed, then evaluation time is not the time to pass final judgment. Analyze your own performance as a manager before moving to evaluate employees' performances under your direction. Do not hesitate to apologize for your own deficiencies in making goals and expectations known.

- Do not write and run. Communicate in person with the employee, and give allowance for him or her to share a personal perspective of what has occurred. Sharing of these perspectives, whether agreed or disagreed upon ultimately, can help to shape the manner in which expectations should be framed for the future.

Constantly recall: management is not a policing function, but an encouraging, developing and coaching function. The performance of employees is often and largely a reflection of the management that they have been provided. Communication is the oil that allows the machinery of management to operate smoothly.

HIRING NEW WORKERS

As absolutely important as the evaluation of existing workers is (and it is!), it is perhaps an even greater responsibility, as well as opportunity, to bring new workers—the right workers—into the environment. Dealing with the hand that you have been given is an essential; choosing the cards with which to play is an advantage. The power of choice when it comes to hiring is a privilege indeed.

There are many schools of thought when it comes to the approaches to hiring, the techniques of interviewing and the evaluation of applicants. All of them will agree, though, that finding the right workers to add to your force is a great challenge, complete with a variety of challenges. "Getting the right people on the bus" is not as easy as it may seem. The size of the potential work force, and the relatively few number of available jobs, breeds a need among applicants to flood as many CVs onto the scene as possible, with hopes that landing a great interview may result in a good job. They may or may not be qualified. They may or may not make any sense at all for the position in question. They will, however, show up in your search!

Should hiring be within your portfolio as a manager, it will be your job to sift through the probable plethora of applicants, find the most promising and appropriate, and then weed through those to find the best answer to your organization's needs. The environment of your work place, productivity of your group, excellence in achievement and overall success in meeting your objectives and goals in the future, rests squarely in your ability to choose correctly. No pressure!

Here is a good beginning point in the launch of your search for new candidates. We have already quoted Jim Collins' assertion that "getting the right people onto the bus" is the main objective in hiring new people. Whereas most organizations and their managers will tend to see positions first, and then attempt to find persons to fill those preconceived positions, it is his contention, with which we agree, that having the right people and building them into a team of vibrant workers (where individual positions may vary, change and adapt according to the demands of the immediate tasks) is a better approach. Having the ability to hire great people, and then build the processes and procedures of work around their gifts and abilities will yield greater results in the end. Of course, this does not mean that you are not looking for people with the right credentials and experience in their fields. We simply assert that, capable people who are willing to be flexible and fluid in their daily work portfolios in order to achieve common goals, will be more dynamic and productive than those who are simply filling preconceived slots, no matter how capably. When such a scenario is possible, it is full of dynamic potential, especially under the guidance of a gifted and creative executive. Of course, there may not always be that potential. In whatever case you find yourself as a manager, however, there are some commonly regarded factors that may help guide your search. Remember, there are always exceptions to the rules, but they should truly be the exceptions.

- **Start with attitude**. Abilities are important, but attitude is more important. Nothing is of greater concern, really, than the characteristics which your new hire is bound to bring into the mix at the office. The person with the right attitude will bring a higher level of input, be more accepted by coworkers, and therefore bring a greater capacity for productivity. (Remember the Michael Jordan affect!) People can be trained to perform, but they must be willing to be trained. "Teachability" is ultimately greater than advance knowledge. Character traits such as the willingness to learn, positive approach, friendly demeanor, cooperative in nature; these will ultimately get you further than the appropriate degree from the right school, or the "x" number of years experience.

- **Check for work ethic**. In most cases, satisfying the attitude concerns mentioned above will cover this concern as well, but it bears repeating nonetheless. Minimal experience or a lack of adequate training can be overcome. The person willing to learn and capable of learning will quickly move beyond those challenges. Even in the case where there exists a need for an employee to hit the ground running, you will quickly find your work advanced more by this person than by the one who seems immediately ready to fit the need, but comes with the wrong attitude. There is no prior training, no credential that can either prove, or remove the need for a proper work ethic. The person who comes to work ready to contribute, positively and expectantly, will boost your results as a manager, and make the journey more pleasant in the process.

- **Seek creativity and intelligence**. You are not simply looking for a work horse, although there may be times and situations where such credentials apply. What you are looking for is the person who gets work done because he *can* get work done. He can take initiative when appropriate, think through issues and find solutions. He is not stopped by the first obstacle that stands in the way of his objective(s), but finds solutions and implements them. We have used the slogan before, "work smarter, not harder." This advice applies to hiring as well.

- **Showcase responsibility**. The person who is never responsible, always shifting blame, always looking for scapegoats, no matter how smart or full of potential, is not the person for you. You can pursue this in an interview by asking about past successes and failures at previous places of employment. Is every questionable aspect of past performance always described as the fault of another, or of unfortunate circumstances? The person that believes herself accountable to her tasks and the overall success of the group will serve you and the organization well. Try to discern what level of responsibility she will accept.

- **Identify non-cooperative individuality**. While not a fault in itself, and sometimes even a characteristic of creativity, the person who insists on his or her individual concerns and perceived rights, who demands latitude from the beginning for pet issues, or who indicates a territorial attitude is a big red flag. Modern work environments, much like modern management, demand team work and cooperation. Synergistic models of fewer people producing more work through creative solutions and grand ideas are at work in today's environment. The lone ranger will only create blockages.

- **Ask for longevity**. People are on the move today. The job force is fluid, with people changing jobs much more frequently now than just a few years ago. The position immediately available may in fact be a stepping stone to greater things, but proper attention to the immediate position must not be lacking! You need people who are planning to stick around, develop together and move the company forward. You need team players who want to see the team succeed, not simply find themselves a better position on another team.

Do not just review... interview!

Again and again, we repeat, *communication is essential!* Decisions of such importance can not be made by studying details contained in job applications or resumes. The diligent manager entrusted with the task of hiring is going to know that the best way to *hire people* as opposed to *filling positions* is going to be the face-to-face communication process. Setting aside enough time to properly meet and interview candidates will help him in getting the right person. Even the conduct of friendly conversations will serve the process well, as the interaction opens the door to revelations and perceptions that might not otherwise emerge.

There are keys to great interviews to which the astute manager should adhere. The manner in which you conduct an interview will go a long way to establishing your ongoing relationship, should the applicant ultimately get the job. It will also be crucial to organizing the environment to either get the best out of the interview process, or to reduce its effectiveness.

A good interview can be birthed out of a good outline. If you are prepared, as you should be, ahead of time, this simple outline can streamline your interaction with the candidate.

1. **Prepare.** Review for your interview! Start with the knowledge that the best results will only come through proper preparation. Walking into interviews with an improvisational attitude will yield rather impulsive and potentially ineffective results. You and your organization can not afford such risky potential, therefore you should take these suggestions into account:

    • You must review the resumes or CVs of applicants prior to the interview in order to be prepared.
    • You must be completely comfortable and knowledgeable with the expectations of the job

that you are filling. You can not add and subtract to the expectations later, once the job is filled. You must be fully informed.

- You must have your questions ready before the interview. (We discuss this more below.)
- You must make ready a proper meeting place for the interview in order to create the most open environment possible for discussion.
- You must have all of the tools necessary for conducting the interview with you: candidate's files, notebook and writing utensils, etc. Do not have to go searching for these items once the interview has begun.

2. **Welcome**. This includes your initial formalities and greetings. Your welcome should be conducted warmly, bringing the applicant into a comfortable setting. You want to create as much freedom of interaction and communication as possible, so it is imperative to present yourself as an open and inviting interviewer. You do not want to take a lot of time in this process—thereby indicating that your time, and that of your interviewee, is valuable—but enough time to set the tone for what is to come.

3. **Introduce**. You should have prepared yourself and your plans for the interview ahead of time with a clear, concise description of the job. Since you are concerned with hiring the right person, and not simply filling a job opening, you will want to include a brief description of the kind of person you are seeking to hire. Remember that it is not your job to sell the position to an applicant, so keep the introduction simple, and honest! Talking up a job beyond its real expectations in order to secure the

interest of an applicant that you like is both dishonest and potentially explosive when expectations are failed.

4. **Question**. Ask the questions that you have prepared to get the right kind of person with the right credentials into this job. This will, of course, include questions of education and experience, the desires and expectations of the applicant, as well as a frank discussion regarding the strengths and weaknesses (at least as they are perceived) of the applicant. How has all of this served him or her in past job experiences? How do they see it applying to this current, potential job? Remember to keep questions as short and pointed as possible, and allow the applicant the lion's share of the time to provide answers. In the questioning process, it is actually more valuable to be a listener than an inquisitor. You will learn much more about the candidate listening to the answers than in describing the job and its expectations, etc.

You would do well to take special notice of the fact that questions must focus on the candidate's ability to perform the job, and not on personal information that is non-relevant to that process. In many instances, especially within developed countries, there are legal concerns as to what questions may and may not be asked. *It is imperative that you make yourself familiar with these restrictions in order to keep yourself and your organization free from liability!* Of course, different environments may require different character traits, and concern for the character of an applicant is not inappropriate! But the manager must exercise propriety.

QUESTIONS TO EXPLORE

a. **Why are you here?** What is it about this place that attracted you?

b. **What can you do for us?** What do you have to contribute to what we do?

c. **What distinguishes you from other people who can do this same job?**

d. **Will you fit in?** Will you get along with, or irritate, all my other employees? And,

e. **Can I afford you?** (It may not be at the time of the first interview, but at some reasonable time in the process, you should communicate the associated salary expectations.)

From www.jobhuntersbible.com

---

5. **Conclude**. Once you have satisfied your need for any information or interaction, give the applicant an opportunity to add information that he perceives to be relevant, or to ask questions that he feels would help him to discern his own fit for the job. Be keen to listen and note any questions or comments, because these items will also serve to introduce you to the capabilities, thought processes and interests of the applicant. Once finished, end the interview politely and provide as much complete and frank information as you can as to when the applicant can expect to hear from you or the organization.

The initial interview will, of course, not be the end of the process in most situations. You will need later to:

* **Review the candidates** by sorting through your notes from the interviews (which of course you were diligent to take!) and revisiting resumes, if necessary.

Rank candidates in order of potential for this position. You will want to work from the top to bottom of your rankings when bringing candidates back for subsequent interviews.

- **Follow up on all possible references**, whether supplied in the application, on resumes, revealed during the interview, or available to you through other search means. Be as thorough as time and ability allow you to be, while recognizing that the careful process of hiring is essential to your organization's success!

- **Conduct subsequent interviews**. If your organization is large enough to accommodate the process, preliminary interviews may be conducted by lower level managers, with the top candidates being passed along until meeting with the decision-making manager.

- **Take the time** to choose the right person. We will continue to strongly advocate this component of the hiring process. If the right person is not revealed through your initial search processes, then look for alternative solutions until the proper person may be found. Hiring the wrong person will create more problems for you and ultimately set you back further than will waiting out the process for its satisfactory conclusion.

If you want your group, department, project or company to succeed, then do not make hiring the least important factor of your job. We started this book on the premise that the requirements of management are more about people in today's jobs market than simply the supervision of the work. If it is about the *people*—at least if you want to be working with the best and brightest— then you shall have to make the issue of hiring a top priority when the need presents itself.

Search actively!

So, where do you find such quality people as you desire? It is almost an iron-clad truth that capable people will not simply—"poof"—appear before you. The task of finding the right people, and giving the appropriate amount of time to the process, means actively searching for the best possible candidates. Remember, it is only the success of your company goals that hang in the balance! Bringing in the right people is bound to encourage, enhance and propel the work that is being done by others, embellish the work atmosphere and generally help to move all things forward. On the other hand, introduction of the wrong person may have negative results that extend far beyond your immediate comprehension. From the consequences to the work, through to the damage that can be created in and among other employees, having the wrong people around can complicate things in ways that will have long lasting affect. You do not want to be responsible for that result!

Like all that we have discussed, experiencing success in any goal or objective, including that of hiring, requires a healthy process. You need a plan to search for the right people. We offer a few suggestions. Each of them may be a valuable source, and some may be more advantageous than others in given situations. All together, they form a solid basis for a thorough search of available candidates.

- **Internal searches**. If we were to prioritize these sources, we would certainly place this one at the top of the list. It is always good to search initially from within the organization, for many reasons: internal workers already understand the values and culture of the organization, high morale is generated among employees who know that the organization values each worker enough to search there first, and the generally less expensive process.

- **Internet recruiting and job bank websites.** Because we are concentrating on modern management, we must list this resource quickly, and move it to the top of the list of your search tools. More and better sites are being created every day, and the internet has distinct advantages to other recruiting outlets. It is often less expensive, provides almost unlimited space for detailing the job and your company, and allows for the information to be available at all times on all days. Savvy applicants—and most notably, computer literate applicants—will be searching for jobs on the internet, and so you are more likely to hook up with such candidates in this way. A potential disadvantage, even more so than using traditional job adds, is that you will likely end up with an enormous number of applicants to sort through.

- **References from respected sources**. While many people bemoan the familiar system of hiring that often degenerates into "who you know" opportunities for getting jobs—as opposed to hiring based on talent and ability—it is nevertheless true that personal references from sources that you respect must be high in your sights as you search. Beware, though, that such personal referrals should be for candidates with whom the person providing the referral is *actually knowledgeable*. The point is that you are gaining the insights and opinions that this contact can provide to you in order to aid your examination of the candidate, not that you are simply expanding the good old boy system.

- **Professional and worker associations**. Usually, the associations that work on behalf of certain professions or groups of workers have resources such as newsletters, magazines, websites and other means of communication through which you can make positions known.

- **Recruitment agencies**. Especially when you are pressed for time in your search for an employee to fill a specific position, employment and temporary employment agencies may be a help to you. The fees that are associated with using such services may be a barrier if funds are not available for your search efforts, especially in the case of permanent employment agencies (or, what are often called "headhunters"). Temporary agencies are a little more flexible, and generally have more accommodating fees. But they will not very often be of great value when dealing with top posts in your organization.

The services, background and reputation of the agency intended for use should be carefully examined. And recall that the primary effort is to find the right *person*, not only an answer to the job opening. For this reason, the impersonal, second hand nature of utilizing employment agencies should not be considered the first option. (Although using "temps" can give more opportunity for getting to know potential permanent workers, if properly utilized.)

- **Job advertisements in newspapers and other periodicals.** This method will certainly get the word out broadly, but such wide distribution of the opening is not always the answer to getting the right people. In fact, you will probably spend much time and effort looking through piles of applications and resumes that are far from being in line with your posting. The job advertisement should be as specific and clear as possible in outlining the qualifications needed, and the responsibilities expected to be shouldered by the candidate.

Whatever methods you choose to engage, the imperative is that you spend appropriate time and energy finding the right person for your company. Filling posts too quickly or out of expediency are not long term solutions to your needs. The quality manager will do what is necessary and allow for the time needed to find the worker your company deserves.

INSPIRING PRODUCTIVITY

The time was that employees were much more inclined to be committed to their work, satisfied in having a job to perform for which adequate compensation was received, and inclined to follow instructions more on the basis of "what" the worker is to do, as opposed to "why" he or she is supposed to do it. Times have changed. The days of unchallenged instructions are largely gone. Today's worker is accustomed to the question, "why?"

So, too, the manager's days of speaking, seeing and judging are over. The days of inspiring and motivating have arrived. Management today, as we have repeatedly stated, is a people task more than a project task. People *need* to appreciate their job, and they *need* to know that the job appreciates them. Performance, more than ever, is linked to job fulfillment and motivation.

As always, positive and negative reinforcements are the tools of the trade. The real shift in management, however, is in the increasing importance of the positive (rewards) and the increasingly detrimental results of the negative (disciplines). The ebb and flow of the work force has created an atmosphere in which workers will choose to move on if they do not feel appreciated or satisfied in their work; especially, those who are capable of locating and moving on to other posts. This means that, should you desire to keep your best, you must learn to create the environment that will do so.

The abundance of management books today will trumpet this simple truth: *you must reward good work.* In fact, you will find yourself as a manager required even to reward what you might classify as nominal work at times. *The issue will be to what extent you reward what behavior.* Little contribution or accomplishment should be little rewarded, while great contributions will be greatly rewarded. But this positive form of reinforcement will be your primary tool. The key is learning how to wield such powerful weapons as rewards and disciplines (positive and negative reinforcements). To do so, you will want to gain knowledge to help: *knowledge of your employees, of their expectations, of key motivators which drive them, and of the rewards that will benefit them.*

1. **Knowledge of employees.** To begin working the people side of your job, you must first come to an understanding of who it is that you are working with. Or, to put it in question form, "What is an employee to you?" Your own attitude in approaching workers is the first building block.

WHAT ARE EMPLOYEES?

Assets? No... assets are depreciated. They have a useful life and then are discarded. You know exactly how much value you will get out of an asset (at least in accounting terms). When was the last time you knew exactly what you were going to get out of an employee?

Capital? No... capital is exchanged. When was the last time you got a group of employees together and sold them to a competitor for a price? Or, better yet, when was the last time you saw the value of a knowledge worker listed on the balance sheet?

Investments? No... when you invest you make an explicit risk / reward calculation. When was the last time you heard a hiring manager say of a new hire "Well, they will probably really mess up the whole project, but if they get it right we are golden!" If employees were investments we would seek to reduce all possible risk for the return we get. Small problem: human beings tend not to do well when managed for risk. They like to be inspired for return.

Volunteers? Closer, but still no. In most organizations the expectations of volunteers is low. The expectation of employees is usually more than "try to show up when you can".

> ***No... employees are investors***. They provide you
> with something of value and you in turn give them a
> return. You want the good ones to give you more and
> the bad ones to give you less. As a manager you
> [want the best people possible to be investing].
>
> **Adapted from www.talentism.com**

Your attitude about the people working with and for
you will shape the manner in which you approach
them on a daily basis and will inform your overall
performance reviews. Mangers today need to see
themselves as people handling some of the most
important investments of their organization: the
people who work there. They are not just means to
an end—tools of the trade—but valuable contributors
toward the goals of accomplishing corporate ends!

2. **Knowledge of expectations**. The communication of
   expectations (does that sound familiar to you yet?) is
   so very important in the work environment today.
   But this is not limited to the expectation of managers
   of their employees. It must include the employees'
   desires for the work place and for their own job
   performance, if they are indeed to be investors in the
   organization. You must create ways to learn and
   inform yourself of what those expectations are, and
   create realistic ways of either meeting them, or
   challenging them in open and collaborative ways to
   bring about other expectations.

3. **Knowledge of key motivations.** Perhaps nothing is
   more important to you as a manager than the skillful
   ability to discern, and more, to in fact implement
   those things which motivate your employees to
   higher levels of performance than those achieved at

prior times. This responsibility, therefore, requires some real attention.

A number of recent surveys have revealed that monetary compensation is moving down the list (unbelievably!) of key motivations. Less tangible issues of job satisfaction are moving closer to the top of the lists. Employees as collaborators need to feel that their contributions matter, that they are noticed and appreciated, and that it earns respect from both coworkers and supervisors alike. That being said, the quest becomes one of keeping workers feeling motivated and productive. How do you do that?

As a player in competitive, college basketball, our team once visited the training camp of a much larger school, with a well-accomplished coach. Many lessons emerged from that few days so long ago, but one particular event stuck with me indefinitely. During a scrimmage practice, one of the senior, veteran players of the other team had possession of the ball, and in a streak delivered a pass to one of his teammates, a freshman recruit. It was a thing of beauty. It was unbelievable that player was even able to see his teammate through the mass of activity, no less deliver such a perfect pass directly to his hands. As he was not expecting the pass, however, the ball bounced off the younger player and out of bounds. A tremendous play was blown. But it was what happened next that captured my attention.

In an instant, the coach was on the floor, his voice raised and barking out corrections. Nothing new for coaches! What was impressive, however, was the player to which the correction was directed. The coach's tirade was unleashed upon the senior who delivered the pass, rather than the freshman who had missed it. What was his reasoning for such a seemingly misdirected rebuke? "You are the leader here! You have the experience! You are controlling the play. *You must know your teammates!* And you must play to their abilities."

Instructor in issues of corporate values, Edgar Schein, outlined in his book, *Career Anchors: Discovering Your Real Values* the idea that each employee has some core issue, a prime motivation that anchors him to the feeling of fulfillment in his job. It is in discovering and utilizing these factors—knowing your players—that you can find the way to best work with and supervise those under your care. It allows you to know the best manner of communication with each employee, as well as to know what positive and negative reinforcements will pull out best performances. Dr. Schein's anchors are outlined below, but whether or not you choose to subscribe to his exact list, the key remains that you need to identify that which truly motivates your workers, and utilize that knowledge to shape the way in which you lead them.

The Eight Anchors

a. **Technical/functional competence**. This person exhibits a simple desire to excel in a particular line of work. Being the best possible in his particular field, arriving at new approaches and solutions, etc., motivates him to perform more than compensation or other particular rewards do. Ongoing learning is important to him in order to stay sharp. He wants to be treated as an expert in his field, and wants to interact with people who are equally knowledgeable. By all means, he does not want to be challenged by those who are not skilled in his field and will not look well upon the manager who feigns knowledge, or can not refrain from speaking about what he or she does not truly understand.

b. **General managerial competence**. This person's sense of advancement is broader than that of the person with technical competence. He might be more of a "jack of all trades," exhibiting competence and confidence in a variety of functions. He will seek to excel in the sense of the corporate ladder, looking for promotions as rewards. People skills are a solid part of his toolbox, and communication is very important to him. He needs to feel challenged by seeing bigger and more responsible projects or jobs placed into his care. If increased financial compensation and job promotions are not rewards that can be made available to him, it will be important for the manager to find other ways of expressing similar kinds of approval. "If I could give you more, I would." Having the confidence of superiors is important to him, and therefore must be communicated to him.

c. **Autonomy/independence**. This person is looking for the flexibility and freedom to do a job that ultimately provides her with her sense of competence. Titles, promotions and increases will mean less to her than that freedom. Actions will speak louder than words, and so being left alone to do the job will mean more to her than constant communication, which might alternatively be perceived as intrusiveness. It will be the manager's challenge to find ways to accommodate this freedom and still find standards of performance measurement. Scheduling *set times* and keeping to them will be most effective. She will not want to be interfered with in between, and that lack of interference will speak volumes in terms of her perception of having been rewarded.

d. **Security/stability**. This person is organizational and systematic. Clear job descriptions, solid policies, and well-defined procedures will help this person to function responsibly and comfortably. She will desire to be in constant communication with supervisors, especially to know that her job performance is perceived as competent. She wants job security, and in the absence of being able to guarantee that, the manager will need to find other ways of keeping contact, reinforcing the perception of value that she brings to the organization, and recognizing loyalty.

e. **Entrepreneurial creativity**. This person is often driven by the feeling of something new and needs constantly to be meeting new challenges. Boredom can set in quickly, and creativity needs to be encouraged. Providing this person freedom to come up with new ideas, and forums in which to share them, is key. He will want to be rewarded with both compensation and promotions in order to feel that he is advancing.

If this can not be offered, public expressions of approval and accomplishment will become increasingly important. Criticisms are best communicated in private chambers.

f. **Sense of service**. Particular values and a sense of a cause to advance will motivate this person. He needs to feel that what he is doing is contributing to that higher purpose. It is, therefore, the manager's task to be highlighting that contribution. When speaking about work issues, they should be tied to the greater concerns of the organization and the values that are at stake. Speaking together as often as possible about the elements of the job that are important to him. It is important to limit his particular assignments to those areas of personal concern, which is an action that will be perceived as reward.

g. **Pure challenge**. "Just give me a challenge and let me go!" will be this person's mantra. She needs to climb, and she needs to excel. She may be quite verbal about things, and will not generally shy away from confrontation. It is not out of bounds for the manager to exercise a bit of confrontation in return, being cautious not to let the interaction culminate in negativity. It is important to require explanations for her answers to inquisitions. The manager will need to keep her moving from assignment to assignment as each one comes to an end, and provide her with as much authority in the proceedings as possible. The assignment of responsible work will be much reward to her.

> ### *Now, Discover Your Strengths*
> An additional, excellent resource toward recognizing
> employee strengths can be found in the work of
> Marcus Buckingham and Donald Clifton.
>
> "Effectively managing personnel--as well as one's own behavior--is an extraordinarily complex task that, not surprisingly, has been the subject of countless books touting what each claims is the true path to success. That said [this work] does indeed propose a unique approach: focusing on enhancing people's strengths rather than eliminating their weaknesses. Following up on the coauthors' popular previous book, *First, Break All the Rules*, it fully describes 34 positive personality themes the two have formulated (such as Achiever, Developer, Learner, and Maximizer) and explains how to build a "strengths-based organization" by capitalizing on the fact that such traits are already present among those within it.
>
> "You can't lead a strengths revolution if you don't know how to find, name and develop your own."
>
> **-- Adapted from a review at www.amazon.com**

h. **Lifestyle**. This person organizes all things around his private life. His most pressing concern is for the job to give him the freedom to balance other concerns—family, hobbies, outside interests—with his work, and he will accomplish what is necessary to provide that (and perhaps little else). The manager will need to be quite clear in outlining performance expectations, responsibilities, rewards and penalties with him, and the greatest reward may be free time at the end of a job well done. If the company allows the manager the freedom to operate on the basis of positive accomplishment of assignments rather than real time spent at work (the job gets done regardless of the time that it takes to achieve that end), this could add to the person's sense of a job well done, while providing additional freedom as a reward.

Ultimately, finding what makes your workers function best will serve you every bit as much as it does them. Allowing employees to work to their strengths and minimize the weaknesses will only boost your work environment, which invariably results in increased productivity. It will serve your people and will building strength into the organization.

4. **Knowledge of rewards**. If positive reinforcements are your primary tool for motivating employee performance, as we have asserted, then it stands to reason that you must be competent in handling these tools. Just throwing rewards around will not gain any more productivity (or trust!) than the failure to use them at all. In fact, many managers are rather ignorant in discerning where, when and how to apply rewards. Often, what appears to be a reward can produce just the opposite, and failures to correct poor performance can become what amounts to rather ineffective rewards. The wise manager will carefully discern between them.

As an example, you may consider the managerial approach applied by a certain supervisor to the situation in which two employees are working under his oversight. One is diligent, competent, and almost always exceeds expectations. The other is a minimalist, doing only what is required, and often not too well at that. Both of them are given assignments to complete. The first comes in with a product early, under budget and with a healthy result. He earns a pat on the back and a quick movement to a new assignment because, well, he is capable and the company needs his contribution. This one is getting things done! The second worker comes in late, having strung the project out, and has just barely met the budget. His effort has only managed to provide a minimal result. His product needs to be improved, so being in a proverbial hurry, the manager takes his project, gets some other employee to help to improve it, and sends the worker along his way.

So what were the rewards? Mr. Diligent Worker was handed a handshake and a new pile of work, while Sub Par Worker was let off the hook and allocated extra resources (another employee) to accomplish the task that he should have delivered in the first place. *The manager may have mentally missed the entire affair, but in fact was responsible for rewarding lazy, incompetent work while actually penalizing the employee who excelled.*

What we learn from the example is clear: the manager must be aware of the manner in which she is reinforcing, whether positively or negatively, the work that her employees are contributing. *Rewards must be based on actual performance, and not arbitrarily or hastily handed out.* The manager must be astute enough to recognize how an individual employee's performance has advanced the work objectives and goals of the team. This is not a matter of mere numbers, but an assessment of how an employee has affected every aspect of work life. What would be worse, or less effective, if this employee were not present? What would be better? What is his or her real contribution?

Whether it is through performance measurements that are clear, such as increased output or cost savings, etc., or through lesser visible aspects of work life, the employee must be noticed for the day to day contribution that he or she makes to the team and to the organization as a whole. Remember: there are very few "break through" moments in which an employee is going to show outstanding achievement. Much of the time, each one is coming in to perform a daily routine. Consistent, small tasks make up the picture of the larger work day; each work day, then, contributing to the profitable work cycle. You can not reward employees only for the break through. They must be appreciated for the work that they perform as a whole.

What should be considered a reward? It is amazing that what is so common to each of us is so often overlooked in the environment of the job. The most obvious form of reward at work, of course, is monetary in nature. After all, that *is* why most of us are there: to earn money. Money, though, is not the only—and most would say not even the most important—of rewards. In fact, many in modern management would caution us that money is the least of all reward motivators in this regard, because paychecks and pay raises have become *expected*. They are the "right" rather than the "recognition".

Increased paychecks are nice, for sure. But when it comes to human nature, we also appreciate the praise. It is recognition, the private as well as the public kind, that makes the heart glow.

A good manager will devise creative *and real* ways of expressing gratitude to workers. From the smallest items so consistently performed to the break-throughs on those grand assignments, people who have performed well need to be recognized and appreciated. And they need to be recognized by their supervisors, not by some distant source that reportedly exists "out there" somewhere. People want to know that their work has been noticed by those working with them, and the immediate supervisor is the most effective source of praise. Certainly, it is nice at times to pass the word up the chain and to bring in support from higher-ups to add weight to the praise. But in the end, employees know that, aside from the break through events, their daily contribution is known by those they work with and for, not by the higher forces. While most people will not require the accolades of the masses to feel fulfilled, they will yearn for the recognition of those closer to their sphere of work and influence. They will desire for those who *should* know to indicate that they *do* know.

As a means of some practical assistance in dealing with these issues, you may consider the following areas. I will by no means suggest that this list is comprehensive, but it can provide you with a handy place to start. These are suggestions adapted from the newsletter of AMP Management.

a. Recognize meritorious behavior.

When employees excel in any regard, move quickly to show your approval and appreciation. Notice such items as:

- Learning new skills
- Showing extra effort to help a co-worker
- Mediating a conflict
- Volunteering for menial work
- Giving a customer extra attention
- Mentoring a new employee
- Tackling a problem in a fresh way
- Making people laugh in a stressful situation
- Sharing information
- Taking notes in a meeting
- Perfect attendance
- Adapting willingly to change
- Cross-training another employee

b. Devise good, non-monetary rewards for excellence.

Remember that, since these rewards do not cost, at least in terms of money, they should be used as frequently as possible when they can be applied meaningfully. They should not be thrown about carelessly, but frequently. Be honest, sincere and generous with your praise, and be equally generous with the privileges available to you as a caring manager.

- A manager will do the employee's job for a day.
- Choice of late arrival or early leave-taking for one day

- A work-at-home day
- Morning coffee & bagel for a day or a week, delivered by a manager
- Three-hour lunch break for one day
- A day off
- Casual dress (if the policy doesn't already exist)

Reward outstanding achievements or consistent excellence with:

- Increased authority. Empower the employee to make monetary decisions, take actions without your signature, or supervise others.
- Designate the person as a project leader, with the opportunity to select other members of the team.
- "Pick your project." Allow the person to determine the next assignment he will work on, within a predefined budget.
- Swap a task. Reward a co-worker with an offer to trade for a day (or a week) a task of yours she covets for one of hers she dislikes.
- A day to work solely on a favorite task. Arrange for coverage of the employee's other tasks so that he doesn't return to a backlog the next day.
- Recognize a team accomplishment by designating that team a consultant to other teams. Team members get the honor and others get the benefit of their skills. You may want to provide them with some training in internal consulting skills.
- "How Can We Help?" Day. A way for a team to show esteem for an overburdened, under-

recognized worker. Each person offers to assume one task for the person being recognized.

c. Create means of formal recognition.

- Write a letter to the employee's family expressing appreciation for extra hours the employee has given to the job, and explaining specifically what he has done and what it means to the company.
- Arrange for a thank-you call from the president of the organization.
- Arrange for a visit from the president to acknowledge the contributions of an individual or a team.
- Put together a thank-you letter signed by everyone in the work unit, framed if you wish.
- Call attention and make an announcement when someone accomplishes a personal goal.

It is important to remember that both top and poor performers need recognition. It's easy for managers to take the top performers for granted, with the assumption that they don't really need external motivation. Poor performers need to be recognized for any small, positive improvements they make, so that good behaviors are encouraged and reinforced.

In the end, you hold major influence as a manager over the experience of your employees, and ultimately in their performance within the organization. As you come to terms with that, you will find yourself not only much more aware of your employees, but playing the part of a positive, contributing force in their progress.

Using the greatest assets in your personal arsenal—time and direct attention—you are ready be that positive and powerful influence.

DEVELOPING, COACHING AND MENTORING

One of the highest ranked ways of showing appreciation and rewarding employees is to show an interest in them that extends beyond their individual product performance. Workers that feel they are being motivated and pushed beyond their current level of expertise or accomplishment are overwhelmingly likely to harbor a sense of fulfillment. There is no greater expression of that level of care than through the development of programs and mentoring opportunities that you are able to provide.

By now, you have certainly noticed that there can be a daunting amount of information to remember, no less attempt to implement, in order to be called an effective manager. Of course, the goal is for these things to become second nature. But here is a hint at a great starting point: employees will forgive a lot of managerial failure in some of these areas when they have been developed, or continue to be developed, by caring managers who illustrate that their interest is taken to heart. When they have not simply been hired and then sent out on their own to wade through the job and the organization, then you will find a force willing to work with you through highs and lows.

The personal interest that you, and through you the organization, take in each employee will propel you to better days. But it must be a committed effort: a real part of your organizational culture. While you can not force employees to improve and develop beyond their present situations, it is imperative that, in the least, you are setting the example and creating an environment that encourages ongoing learning and growth. Most will follow suit.

This term "environment" is important. While seminars, programs, classes and the like will certainly fit into your development programs, it is the day to day activity within the company that has the most affect. Your primary task is to create the atmosphere that makes people want to grow, and in which the opportunities are there to be taken advantage of.

If you have taken the task of performance evaluations to heart (see the first section of this chapter), then you are already at an advantage and well on your way. As stated then, correct performance review is not a once-off thing. It is an ongoing process, from beginning to end of any project or objective. As you are watching over employees during that process, you are supplying feedback, encouragement, training and other essentials to help them succeed in the objectives. This is the lion's share, a tremendous step forward, in achieving the kind of personal development that you are hoping to provide. We will not rehash all of these elements. If you are not fresh on them now, go back and do a quick review, because we want to build on this premise in order advance the quest for employee development. Consider now the advantages in this pursuit.

To being with, there are tasks that arise each and every day that some people are competent to perform, and others are not. Often times, managers are guilty of giving the wrong assignments to the wrong people, because they are unaware of the actual abilities (or lack thereof) of individual employees. Development programs offer the opportunity to discover these realities, and when possible, to address them with training that brings deficient workers up to par. At least, the right assignments may be issued to the right recipients, thereby freeing up workers and reducing the complications and duplications that so often occur otherwise.

Just as you want to live by the mantra, "Work smarter, not harder," you want your employees to be able to do the same. Smarter work simply, and always, leads to improved performance and greater output. The worker is happier, and the manager—that's you!—is able to work with less stress and fewer interruptions. Your employees are gaining greater perspectives through development, learning new skills that can be applied, thinking in deeper levels and becoming increasingly motivated through the sense of advance! Understanding this, the question should be turned on itself. It is not, "Why should the company have development programs?" but, "Why would any company *not* have such opportunities?"

This also allows for your organization's pool of potential to increase, without hiring anyone extra! One of your core concerns as a manager is that there are people ready, and able, to move into spots that come open as others move up or move on. This includes your own post. As you are increasing performance and productivity within your own department, you are preparing to move up to greater responsibilities. Someone must be ready to step into your spot.

Organizations that do not need to spend countless hours and expend resources on headhunting people to fill spots, especially in higher levels of management or within particularly skilled environments, are provided with a great advantage.

And it is not just a matter of moving into new jobs. You need to be able to leave the office, just as your bosses do, without the concern that things in your area are going to fall apart in your absence following you. While making yourself indispensable sounds like a great idea—and at certain levels it is—being so for particular work loads that must be fulfilled for things to function will only tie you inextricably to your job. You will be forced to forget vacations. Forget the breaks that you have earned. To avoid this, your goal should be focused instead on becoming indispensable as a trainer, motivator and producer of workers that in themselves can not be replaced with equals from the outside!

Put some effort into it!

If management today is about *people*, and it is, then your people are worth the time, energy and expenditure that it takes to develop them in their professional, and personal, growth in the job. Organizations that show such interest are apt to attract the most capable people. Managers that invest in the process are apt to attract the best from among those available from that pool. In your own quest for excellence, you want to be that manager. You want to be stimulating, challenging, inspiring and growing your people, and thereby attracting the best of them to want to work with you. You want to see your levels rise: in productivity, in job satisfaction and in environment.

Now that you are convinced that personnel development is important (or, *career development*, as it is often called), you must start planning the process. Remember that you are the key. You are the manager. Development starts with you, and more, *it will not happen without you*. The future development of your project, your department, your organization, now settles upon you, and you must make a plan. Sure, the employees must help, and you can not make them grow. But still, your role is to be attentive to the need and to the process, and to be the catalyst for seeing development through. Here are three easy guidelines to assist you in meeting that challenge.

1. **Partner with your employees to discern their desires**. No one knows better than you do where you plan to go and what you plan to achieve, and the same is true for your workers. Meet with them to discuss their place in the organization, the roles that they play and the expectations of what they should achieve. Talk together about future career plans. As trite as it may seem, the question still works, "Where do you see yourself five years from now? Ten?" It will be no good trying to force employees in directions that they don't want to go in terms of career path, so you need to know what they think. You know where the company is planning to be in the days and years ahead, and you need to know who is going to be there to help that advance. You need to know if there will by anyone to help, or if others will need to be sought. This two way communication is essential to meeting the needs of everyone: the worker's, your's and that of the organization.

Career development plans may be more formal, and will outline the expectations of training and long-term development, and the steps for achieving each of these, that will provide advancement opportunities for the employee. We could call these career development goals and objectives. Charting a path of education, training and personal development together; clarifying these objectives and communicating the details; and ultimately coordinating together to see them come to pass, are essential processes.

2. **Partner with your employees to discern their needs.** No one knows your abilities and deficiencies better than you do, and the same is true for your workers. You need to meet together to discuss these talents and abilities (or lack of them), and their use to the organization as a whole. You need to analyze and address the strengths that a person possesses, and the weaknesses that hinder him. Remember that you want to spend more time optimizing strengths than developing in areas of weakness. This is opposite to many organization's development techniques, as they constantly try to eliminate deficiencies, or at least raise the bar in areas of weakness in practical terms. While that is not a bad principle, when it comes to the area of individual performance, both the organization and the employee will gain better efficiency and enhanced fulfillment out of playing to the strengths. Minimizing the influence of weaknesses in the work areas will yield better results than spending great amounts of time, energy and resource on training a person in an attempt to eliminate those weaknesses. Development in the areas of weakness is not bad.

On the contrary. But when it comes to allocating the time and resources of the company, it is the true talents and abilities of the individual that will contribute most. Play to the strengths, and minimize the influence of weaknesses.

3. **Partner with your employees to see it through.** Once you have agreed together on plans for improvement, training and development programs, follow through on your side of the commitment. And furthermore, see to it that employees follow through on theirs. Unless heaven and earth move to conspire against it, don't break the agreements that you have made. Give the time, support and resources that are necessary to see it through. Create a mutual accountability for progress that helps development take place.

In our previous discussion of performance evaluations, we mentioned that career development plans could be an included part of that appraisal. There is a benefit to that, in that it ensures that the process will take place at least at those times. The detriment, however, is that there is less time to work on either of the two tasks: performance evaluation on the one side, and career development planning on the other.

How to proceed with that issue is, of course, up to you. But in any event, it is important to the organization and its employees that such development plans do exist, and that the resources necessary to carry them out well are allocated in order to implement them with excellence. The more often that time and opportunity can be applied to this task, the better off each one will be; the better the overall work environment will be.

When possible, personalize it!

The best personnel development does not occur in classrooms, seminars or other such environments. It happens between living, breathing individuals.

When I first left college to take my first post in the "grown-up world," I was privileged to be placed into one of the most pure forms of mentor/apprentice relationships that I have ever had opportunity to personally witness. In fact, the dynamics of the given situation were such that I had not one, but two, intimate mentors at work. These were people that, in many literal ways, I worked, ate, lived, traveled and vacationed alongside. The work that they did, which thankfully was quite advanced and full of achievement, became the work that I did. I was privy to information, people, processes and events that provided me with an education for which I could have never paid. The result was a quick introduction into leadership and responsibility, and, I trust, the ability to achieve in that environment.

There are some who would divide the concepts of *mentoring* and *coaching* into two different spheres. And I do concede the point. Coaches are those, as we will discuss further later on, who are intimately involved in guiding, assessing and helping individuals to excel in their given areas. This is, as we have been arguing thus far, very definitely the role of management. Managers can be mentors, in some regard, to those they oversee, however those of this school of thought will prefer to identify mentors as outside forces who may be turned to for counsel, guidance and, at times, a kind of therapy, apart from the immediate work environment. They are people who are knowledgeable in the field, and willing to share that influence and insight with you for the benefit of your growth and advance.

Whether or not you buy this distinction, the role of the mentor is an indispensable one for both sides of a single equation. First, you, as a manager or potential manager, would greatly benefit from such a force in your life. Not everyone is lucky enough to make that connection with another, but if and when you do, it is something to be treasured. The other side of that equation is that, once you have developed personally, it is equally imperative for you to offer that benefit to another. It serves your own development, as well as that of the recipient, to be engaged in mentoring practices that keep you sharp, and that allow you to increase the results of your life and career through the process of duplication. (It might be argued that this results in *multiplication*, not just *duplication*.)

The benefits of both giving and receiving in the mentoring process are enormous, not to mention socially responsible. Whether provided through formalized mentoring programs within an organization, or through the voluntary, and sometimes even unrecognized, processes of interaction, the mentoring process aids in development in ways that other programs can not. One reason for this, and not least among them, is because of the credibility that is built through personal interaction. The trust of someone who has been there and done that to invest in you, and the trust that you give in allowing someone to feed into your life in that manner, is an explosive ingredient. The training program becomes exponentially purposeful when it is reinforced with such personal relationships.

The inside knowledge of an accomplished teacher, the examples of experience, past trials and victories, and the discussion and guidance that is generated from them are incalculable in their affect in the growth and development of an individual.

As for *coaching in management*, now here is where it gets really personal. Nothing could be closer to the heart, or at least the job description, of a manager. This is at least true in the context that we have laid it out in this book. The word itself gives us enough explanation. We all know coaches to be those people who provide strategies, give guidance and provide for the training needed to advance the cause of their teams. Coaches are not, in essence, the doers of the immediate tasks. They are the implementers, overseers and cheerleaders of the activity. And the same characteristics hold true for the world of management.

> **The mediocre teacher tells.**
> **The good teacher explains.**
> **The superior teacher demonstrates.**
> **The great teacher inspires.**
>
> **--William Arthur Ward**

Someone has said, "Tell me, and I will forget. Show me, and I will remember. But include me, and I will learn." This is a sound management principle. Employees can not be expected to perform by simply being told to go and do, thought that is often the case. Instead, they need to be told, showed and involved, until they have learned the real task. That is where the job of a coach comes in. The following *show and tell* method of training can aid in this approach. The three-fold method has proven itself through generations of management coaching to be quite effective.

1. Describe the task and illustrate how to perform it step by step. (You tell, you show.)
2. Describe the task again, and let the other person perform it step by step. (You tell, they show.)
3. Let the other person perform the task and describe it to you as they go, step by step. (They tell, they show.)

Other than training in specific areas of activity, as we have described above, it might still be asked, "What is the description of a manager/coach?" It is a question with many answers floating around and available through business and educational communities. There are an almost unlimited number of programs that one can follow to learn executive and management coaching techniques. There are full time jobs in the coaching community. There are even coaches of coaches now, and each of them will have an opinion as to what a coach truly does.

In an effort to simply the thought for our purposes here, we will zoom in and focus specifically on the manager who is *coaching workers- people- in the context of his management job, because he sees his job in that context.* He is the manager that we have been describing throughout these pages. He knows that, in order to coach his people, he must provide the four A's of coaching: *availability, advice, acquisitions and acclaim.*

1. **Availability**. When employees are in need of help, he does not see them as an imposition on his day, but *within proper boundaries,* is there to hear the

problems and help as he is able. He is not shielded entirely away from employees by a guard at the door (or what we sometimes call "executive secretaries"), and he is at times out and around the office or work space checking on the condition of his workers.

2. **Advice.** He is able and willing to provide knowledge and input into the work load when it is sought or required. His knowledge and experience, and large picture view of the goals and objectives, give him a platform to speak from. When he has practical knowledge, he is there to share, and beyond that, he is providing the context for the varying parts, encouraging the group members to see how each part plays into the whole. He is there to hear ideas and provide feedback, as well as to offer ideas and seek feedback. He is listening to the challenges and the advances each individual is facing in fulfilling his or her function, sympathizing, admonishing and encouraging along the way.

3. **Acquisitions.** By this, we mean that when the work load is too much, or beyond the abilities of an individual, he is available to help find solutions, get the help that is needed, obtain the resources that are required, and steer workers into the training and development necessary for advance. He is providing solutions to the overload or shortcomings that are sometimes faced by employees.

4. **Acclaim**. Providing encouragement along the way, giving praise for performance and distributing rewards for accomplishment, are some of the most profound offerings a good coach has at his disposal.

Certainly, coaching is a dynamic process. No two workers are the same, and a good manager/coach is able to come to terms with the individuality of each member of his team. This can be accomplished with the help of the discovery of each person's anchor, and imaginatively devising ways to work with the strengths and needs of that individual.

> **The key is not to prioritize what's on your schedule, but to schedule your priorities.**
>
> **-- Stephen R Covey**
>
> **What lies behind us and what lies before us are tiny matters compared to what lies within us.**
>
> **-- Ralph Waldo Emerson**

No greater purpose could be served by the manager than this aspect of people management. Of course, it is still his purpose to help set goals and meet them. Project management, strategy, budgets, performance reviews and so many other elements are going to always compete for the time and resources available to him. But in the end, it is the people working as a part of the team that are ultimately going to make the work happen. They are going to be the largest contributors to the environment in which that is done. It is imperative that the wise, modern manager recognizes that people can not be the last concern in the delegation of his time and attention.

Addendum to Chapter 3
Sample Performance Evaluation

□ Original copy to employee file   □ Copy to employee

Name of Employee:		Department and Division:
Supervisor's Name:	Date Hired:	Period of Evaluation:
Length of time serving under this supervisor:	_____Yrs. _____Mos.	

Performance Evaluation

01 Job Responsibility Rating: □ Superior □ Very Favorable □ Favorable □ Unfavorable □ Unacceptable	Comments
02 Job Responsibility Rating: □ Superior □ Very Favorable □ Favorable □ Unfavorable □ Unacceptable	Comments

03 Job Responsibility	Comments
Rating: ☐ Superior ☐ Very Favorable ☐ Favorable ☐ Unfavorable ☐ Unacceptable	
04 Job Responsibility	Comments
Rating: ☐ Superior ☐ Very Favorable ☐ Favorable ☐ Unfavorable ☐ Unacceptable	

OVERALL EVALUATION	Comments
Rating: ☐ Superior ☐ Very Favorable ☐ Favorable ☐ Unfavorable ☐ Unacceptable	
PLANS FOR DEVELOPMENT: ☐ Personal Development Plan Completed	Comments

EMPLOYEE COMMENTS:

Signature of Supervisor	Signature of Employee
☐ I have conducted this evaluation. ☐ I have discussed this evaluation with the employee.	☐ I have reviewed this evaluation. ☐ I have discussed this evaluation with the Supervisor.
Other Authorized Signature Position:	The Employee signature does not indicate agreement or disagreement with the evaluation, but only what is indicated in the spaces marked above.

Chapter 4
Managing the Team

Earlier in the book, I used the story of my short time on a US ranch to make the point that people, more like horses than cattle, must be led by example. As difficult as horses are to manage in herds, people can be ever so much more challenging. And the manager in today's work environment is not likely to avoid the need to manage teams!

What is a team? Our friend Merriam Webster defines it as "a number of persons associated together in work or activity." Some other guru, unknown to us, has declared it to be, "a distinguishable set of two or more individuals who interact dynamically, interdependently and adaptively to achieve specified, shared and valued objectives." In our simple context, *it is a number of people (more than one) grouped together to work toward specific objectives or goals.*

Teams are dynamic entities, where the skills, abilities, knowledge and creativity of each individual can find expression and contribute to the common effort. The use of teams allows for objectives to *not* be confined by the limitations of a single person performing alone or exercising control over a given enterprise. In terms of management, this compels the manager to find ways to avoid being a source of limitation by exercising so called "control" and instead turn toward the process of collaboration. This social dynamic of collaboration that is so much a part of the modern worker's psyche must be absorbed, assimilated, harnessed and used to the advantage of the organization.

> **"A dwarf standing on the shoulders of a giant may see farther than the giant himself."**
> **-- Didacus Stella**

We will not take a lot of time here to outline the shift in corporate thought that has occurred in the past several years away from what many call *vertical organization* to *horizontal,* or away from the *hierarchical* structures to more—shall we say it again?—*collaborative* ones. The student of management would be well advised to delve into that further. The fact remains, however, that the shift has occurred, and the modern manager is left with the task of forming and leading cooperative efforts.

There are certainly some challenges associated with the shift to address. Among them looms the fact that many of us have been trained in old structures, and that our experience has been in and through them. We still understand well the systems associated with hierarchy, the reports, and the chains of command. We are comfortable with the "say it and expect it" forms of management. While leadership, and accountability, and reporting, and degrees of responsibility are all still pertinent factors, the manner in which much of this takes place has experienced transition.

There are advantages to the changes as well. It is not just the response to social shifts that has caused changes, but also the recognition that the changes can add benefit to the life of an organization, and to the experience of each one working in it. These benefits include such things as more streamlined communication processes coupled with less interference, which has led to more streamlined decision-making processes with fewer bosses to answer to. It has helped to downsize the need for large middle management structures, thereby saving money, and it has moved authority and responsibility for decisions to those with the most to gain or lose by the process. Responsibility rests in much larger part with those who are closer to the point of impact.

The importance of the flow of communication and cross-pollination between varying groups affected by the same decisions and pursuing the same objectives has become indisputable. We see this in every fabric of industry, enterprise and government. At the time I write this, governments around the world, and especially in the Western world, are discussing and grappling with ways to get communication to flow, both between their own departments dealing with common problems, and between the governments themselves who are charged with the responsibility to meet the common challenges of an increasingly globalized world.

We are learning to collaborate. Share rather than compete. Synergize rather than separate. We are commissioned to allow the best qualities of every contributor to benefit the common goal.

FORMULATING, EMPOWERING AND GOVERNING TEAMS

The beginning point is to determine what kinds of teams you need to operate efficiently in your environment. In most corporations, there will be teams that are quite formal and organized, and others that are rather informal and functional. You will need to be aware of which serve the purposes that you wish to accomplish in the pursuit of your goals. For our purposes, we will distinguish between two general forms of teams, which we will call "*standard teams*" and "*project teams*".

1. **Standard teams.** These teams are comprised of various forms and are specially commissioned by executive management to produce specific results within a given performance area. They are more analogous to such standard forms as *committees*, which are very long term or permanent structures that exist for an ongoing task. The members of the committee will change, but the role of the committee remains. Safety committees, steering committees, recognition teams, and management teams are all examples. They tend to be cross-functional, but they also endure over time to support the primary goals of the organization.

2. **Project teams.** These teams, defined commonly by such terms as *task groups* or *process teams*, serve very much like standard teams, but they are constructed for a specific purpose, set out in order to be accomplished within a given timeframe. Once the work of the team is completed, it disbands. They are typically involved with the planning, design or development phase of an objective or goal. Often comprised of people from different departments, they will combine varying perspectives and abilities from diverse participants in order to come to common solutions through, hoperfully, creative processes. Like standard teams, they should have clear goals and roles of responsibility.

Team structures and composition are very important, because it is within the teams that the bulk of communication will take place within your organization. How information flows and to whom are core concerns of the team manager.

However the teams in your department or organization are designed, the effectiveness of the teams, and therefore of the organization you serve, rests in the ability to empower these teams with the proper amount of freedom and authority to function. The danger rests in reverting back to traditional forms of operation under new names: new wine in old wine skins. *Empowerment* means that, once teams have been formulated, they are entrusted with as much authority to function as possible. Decision making abilities, designation of responsibilities within the group, even the choice of leadership: as much as can be delegated to the group should be.

It is universally believed (OK, maybe not *universally*. There are still some old-timers out there!) that such empowered teams inevitably bring better services to those benefiting from an organization, and do it quicker, cheaper and more effectively. It also allows for managers to be released into performance of more of the tasks they generally could not afford to spend time and energy on; such as, the coaching, mentoring, evaluating and developing that we have so far outlined in this book. It elevates the attitudes and morale of workers, and encourages workers to be the investors in the organization that you need to them to be.

The ability of teams to make decisions quicker, arguably better, than was traditionally available through the "get all the information possible to the manager so he can make a decision" process should not be downplayed. Workers are closer to the real challenges that exist within an organization, their communication between one another is more frequent and easily transferred, and therefore the ability to come back with joint decisions is enhanced. The end result is the ability to address needs more quickly and efficiently.

Equally as impressive is the dynamic created by teams that allows for the integration of different perspectives, knowledge, abilities and experiences into a common project. When teams are functioning well, these various characteristics combine to create innovative processes and solutions. The team really is greater than the sum of its parts; their efforts are multiplied rather than added. With less bureaucracy to deal with, teams can function flexibly to meet the challenges that arise and adapt to the changes that occur in the work environment efficiently.

So what really is *empowerment?* The short answer is: *the ability to make decisions, pursue challenges and produce results without too much managerial interference.* And what does that mean practically? Empowered teams are self-sufficient groups of people working together to achieve specific goals. They have the corporate authority, experience, responsibility and skills to enact their own decisions on behalf of the organization. The highest level of management provides the team with directions and limitations, which drives the empowerment process by linking it to the organization's business needs and corporate vision. Management focuses on developing employees and supporting and governing the organizational goals. The employees are committed to, and responsible for, successfully achieving organizational goals. Often times, employees find their job descriptions being redefined and broadened, usually adding some tasks formerly performed by others and losing others less fitted to their abilities. The object is to maximize the use of everyone's talents.

Once the goal has been stated and clarified, the team is left to decide the best ways forward for achieving goals. Team members themselves will:

- Choose their leaders
- Add or adjust responsibilities
- Eliminate non productive team members
- Set the objectives for achieving the goals and assign roles and measurements
- Motivate their own training, and
- Begin and end as a team, with the success of the team as a whole qualifying the success of the individual parts.

Of course, there are challenges to groups which must be addressed and met by managers. They are made of people, and as such, they experience limitations that come with being people-made. The manager-as-coach is concerned with guiding the group as a unit, and not only the individual members that comprise it. He becomes a kind of therapist for work groups!

A phrase that is quite touted in management circles now is that of "self-managed" groups, which might be the ultimate expression of what we have described above. Mark Chatfield of the Interaction Research Institute outlines the differences, however, between self-managed and self-directed teams, which call for some attention.

1. **A Self-Managed Team** is a group of people working together *in their own ways* toward a common goal *which is defined outside the team.* They operate under the guidelines and limitations defined by executive leadership. The team does their own work scheduling, training, granting rewards and recognition, etc.

2. **A Self-Directed Team** is a group of people working together in their own ways toward a common goal *which the team defines.* (Just as above, but the team also handles compensation, discipline, and acts as a profit center by defining its own future.)

Some of the lessons learned in implementing teams:

1. To create a team, a demand for performance is more important than team-building exercises. You can get a group together and train them in teamwork for weeks but they won't be a team until they have a common understanding of the need to perform. First comes the strategic plan, then the tasks needed to carry out the plan, finally, teams are formed to do the tasks.

2. Team basics are often overlooked. Team basics are: size, purpose, goals, skills, approach, and accountability.

3. Teams at the top are the most difficult. Executives have complex, long-term challenges, heavy demands

on their time, and they got where they are by being [individuals].

4. There's no need to throw out the hierarchy. Teams are the best way to integrate across structural boundaries. They are the best way to design and energize core processes.

5. Teams permit performance and learning at the same time. There is no better way to become a learning organization than to have a team-based structure which thrives on people learning from peers. The learning endures.

-- Mark Chatfield, Interaction Research Institute. www.humaninteract.org

COMMUNICATING WITH THE TEAM

Managing can not be done well without great forms of communication. That's right, not just good. Great! The manager who excels will find ways to use all of the tools available to him in order to communicate the message of the moment. And rest assured, there are more forms available, and therefore expected and required for use, than ever before. The information age is upon us, and we have many ways at our disposal to create our communications.

Communication is life-blood to an organization. It simply can not be overstated. Just as the blood brings oxygen and nutrients to the parts of the body that require them, communication gets all of the "stuff" out to the parts of the organization that need it. As a manager, communicating with your team is very much the delivery of the food for energy that is needed to make work happen, and happen well.

> **"Effective communicators remember that 'words have no meaning - people have meaning.' The assignment of meaning to a term is an internal process; meaning comes from inside us. And although our experiences, knowledge and attitudes differ, we often misinterpret each other's messages while under the illusion that a common understanding has been achieved."**
> **— Larry Barker**

First, let's realize that there are both formal and informal types of communication that take place in the work environment every day. Information passes in fast and furious ways. Some of it appears on letterhead, some of it passes at the water fountain. But it is flowing, and it is the harnessing of the processes of communication that will most benefit the manager. And it is harnessing of both the formal *and* the informal processes that will cause one to excel. The reason for this is that, in the modern environment, much of the discrepancies have been leveled. Information passed informally may have as much or more affect than that which is passed formally. Still, there will be times and places in which formal communication will be absolutely required.

Let us not make light of this. A good manager needs to have good communication skills, including formal ones. The abilities to craft a good letter or memo, to speak correctly and intelligently, and even to give a good speech are not passé. Few things speak worse of a leader than the inability to do quality work in the realm of communication. These skills must be honed to the highest degree possible.

The day to day communication of the work environment, however, requires even more. The modern manager must be attuned to a vast array of options. The explosion of technology accompanying the expansion of the information age makes it so. Not only is it necessary because of the tools made available to the manager, but also because of the necessity of being reachable and able to work with those who communicate and function with these tools. Keeping the advantage means possessing the ability to communicate in as many forms as possible. Consider the effects that such tools as these have had upon offices and factories worldwide.

- Email.
- Internet.
- Voice mail.
- Fax machines.
- Cell and video phones.
- Notebook computers.
- Personal Data Assistants (PDA's).

And in the days to come, there are more that are surely to be unveiled. The manager that is behind the technological curve is at a great disadvantage. The ability to move information quickly, cheaply and with great ease is transforming the way that decisions are made, by whom and at what times. It is imperative that the modern manager learns to use all means available him to help make the organization work smarter. From every side, we are assured that this is the key to productivity!

If you are left with little (or no) knowledge or ability to use these items mentioned above, then it is imperative for your own development and career progress that you take the time to explore and learn to use these technologies. Additionally, stay attuned to the developments in technology and communication that are inevitable, and which *may*, and should, be utilized to increase your effectiveness.

It's not just talking!

As it is often said, communication is a two-way street. Learning to communicate effectively with employees, coworkers, customers, bosses or peers requires not only the development of your speaking skills, but of your listening skills.

> **"The most basic of all human needs is the need to understand and be understood. The best way to understand people is to listen to them."**
> **— Ralph Nichols**

Imagine this scenario. A manager has a shortcoming that has caused more than one person to leave his office feeling unappreciated and unheard. Much of his life is spent behind a computer screen, and because of this, it often stands between him and the person that has come seeking help or interaction. The problem is the screen between them. It captures his attention. It keeps him diverted on things other than what the person before him is sharing. (Or, actually focused on them, because it often gets the greater share of his attention!) The visitor is talking, and he's glancing at email. Or worse yet, answering it! The manager lifts his eyes and then again, up pops a message. He glances away again. And this non-communicative dance goes on.

What is the message that the manager is sending in this scenario? The message is not only, "I don't hear you." It is, "I don't care about what you are saying. I don't care why you are here." In short, the person is an intrusion upon what he would rather be doing! He has communicated wonderfully to his worker, first, his own self importance and the priority of his work and life over that of the other person, and then, the fact that he can be wonderfully rude... all at the same time!

It is essential that, when it is time to listen, the good manager is doing just that. He is taking measures to show his interest and to maintain focus on the person with whom he is communicating. He is asking questions to ascertain key points, to clarify statements and to probe further issues. He is listening, most importantly, without illustrating the need to be continually interrupting. And he is showing through his actions, as well as his words, that he is listening, by regulating body movements and facial expressions. When it is appropriate, he is taking notes and communicating those notes back to gain further clarity.

It must be the priority in times of verbal communication to truly understand the message that is being conveyed. That takes effort. Too often, communication can be distorted or misconstrued simply because proper time and effort are not applied to make sure that everyone involved comprehends what is being said and therefore clear on what is taking place. Skilled listening, modeled for other workers, will go far to improve the communication processes within the work place.

One of the most frustrating experiences in the course of the work day is to receive written communications from coworkers that illustrate either a lack of ability, or a lack of care, in the crafting of these documents. Sloppy work, bad form and deficient grammar reveal only one of two things: either a worker does not care to be trained in these skills, or a worker does not care to take the time and effort to properly use skills to create a better product. In the end, the result is a document that says anyway that *the worker does not care.* This may sound like an overstatement to some, however to the person(s) on the receiving end of the communication it is precisely the message that comes across.

Write it well!

Simple care can go a long way in helping you craft effective communication. In today's business environment, you need not be a speech writer or possess a Masters in communication to do this, but you must make appropriate efforts nonetheless. The following thoughts might help.

1. **Write with ease**. In the beginning, write as you would speak. You are not trying to prove your eloquence; you are working to be understood. People understand simplicity, so write it so. (Remember, however, that "simple" and "ignorant" are not synonymous!) Make your points clear, concise and as short as possible.

2. **Read your writing**. Never send written communication fresh from your pen (or fingertips). Before you expect another person to read your ramblings, do so yourself. In fact, do it out loud if you are in an

environment that allows for it. Be attentive to places where you may not have adhered to the guideline above. Look and listen for uncomfortable phrases or crowded thoughts. Remember, you want to be well understood!

3. **Rewrite your writing**. Make the adjustments, and then re-read it again. Keep at it, within reason, until your document flows well, looks good and can speak positively of your skills.

4. **Use technology**. Most of us use computers to create our documents these days, and on these computers run software programs designed to assist us. Use the spelling and grammar tools (usually including a thesaurus) of your specific word processing package to assist you in looking and sounding better.

Present it well!

A presentation is an opportunity for you to bring information to a group of people creatively and informatively, using appropriate tools such as visual aides to do the job well. In order to make solid presentations, you will be well served to review these few tips.

1. **Get organized.** Before a presentation can be prepared, you must be aware of your objectives for the effort at hand. What is it that you are trying to communicate? What do you want to accomplish at the end of the session? Tailor your approach to both the *goal of the presentation,* and *the people* that will be the recipients of the presentation—the audience. Make a few notes for yourself toward answering

these concerns that you can keep as guideposts throughout your time of preparation.

2. **Use the "tell, tell and re-tell" method.** As you are preparing the content of your presentation, begin with the "meat" and then create both your introduction and conclusion around that content. Your goal will be to tell, tell and re-tell; that is,

   a) tell them what you are going to tell them (introduction),
   b) tell them what you are telling them (body), and
   c) tell them what you told them (conclusion).

Your introduction and conclusion should be short, concise statements, or restatements, of the body of content. This repetition serves to both organize your thought flow, as well as to reinforce the points that you are making for the purposes of learning.

3. **Be aware of the whole package.** Content is only a part of the presentation. Having great content will certainly move you well along toward your successful goal, but if it were only about content, you could have written a memo! Presentations are about the content, about the audience, *and* about the presenter. The Cape Higher Education Consortium has offered a couple of helpful charts in this regard.

Tips for Preparation	
Check for grammar and spelling errors	Make sure that your presentation is free of any spelling or grammatical errors. Let someone proofread your work. You don't want to be embarrassed by spelling errors during your presentation.

Practice your presentation	Practice your presentation by yourself or with a friend. Make sure you keep within the time frame allowed for the presentation. The more you practice it before the time, the more confident you will feel when you give the presentation.
Have a plan B	Remember when you make use of slide shows, you are using technology. We all know that technology is not always to be trusted. Have a Plan B ready. For example, have a paper copy of your presentation and transparencies available for emergencies.

Tips for Presentation	
Test your Presentation	Allow time before you start your presentation to test the equipment you are going to use. Familiarize yourself with the set-up. Check the clarity of the content and the colors again, and make changes if necessary.
Introduce yourself	Always introduce yourself and your topic, and briefly explain the process that you are going to follow with your presentation.
Be professional	Your appearance (dress and grooming), the quality of your handouts and your visual presentation, etc., are very important.
Timing	Start promptly and keep within your time frame. Remember to leave enough time for questions afterwards.
Be enthusiastic	Be enthusiastic about your presentation and remember to smile - this will help to relieve some of the stress.
Make eye contact	Remember to make eye contact with your audience. Never read your presentation - this is boring and you will lose the attention of your audience.
Speaking	Speak as loudly and clearly as you can to make sure that all the members in your audience can hear your presentation. There

	is no point in giving a presentation if most of the audience has trouble hearing you. If you struggle to speak louder, make use of a microphone system. Don't speak too rapidly.
Thank you	At the end of your presentation, thank your audience for their time.

Much more detail is provided in the companion book within this series, *Organizational Communication*. We recommend that you acquire and study more intensely the guidelines to effective communication. For now, let us be awakened to the need for such focused and attentive application of efforts to hear and to be heard.

MANAGING THE ENVIRONMENT

Vision statements, communicated goals, developed processes and procedures; these are all tremendous items of value to any organization. As an effective manager, however, you will be well aware that the development of guidelines and their publication are never the end of the story. Every work place has its own environment, and there is a multiplicity of things that converge to create it. In this section, we will touch on some of these more ethereal subjects that conspire to make the job of the manager more interesting.

First, we want to return to the beginning of this book, and the foundational understanding that *employee behavior that would be expected by management, must be modeled by management.* Much of the flow of interaction—while not able to be dictated, and even difficult to call controllable—is down to the example that you generate for your coworkers.

Using the information that is available to you, including,

- Vision and mission statements
- Statements of organizational values
- Organizational charts
- Codes of conduct and behavior
- Other core documents

You will have to make the effort as a conscientious manager to define and organize some of the unique, internal concerns that you must deal with in your own group or department. These will include such things as the ethical conduct of your coworkers and employees, as well as dealing with employee conduct and discipline. What will need to be at the forefront, through both your language and your behavior, is that you are a *principled leader.* You speak and do what you mean. You set the example, and you expect appropriate behavior to follow. It is not simply about *what* work gets done, but increasingly in today's society, it is about *how* that work gets done. And much of that is up to you.

Principled leadership; principled work.

The subject of ethics in the work place has rarely been more front-and-center than it is today. Executives and managers throughout organizations are being required to examine and modify procedures, and the behavior of the people who are carrying them out, through the lenses of a more ethical approach. The term "ethics" can be quite broad, and given the present (and likely, future) environment, somewhat diluted due to overuse, so we will address the issue with this term, *principled* leadership. Principled leadership is that which believes the conduct of the leader, and of those led, is equal in importance to the simple measurements of production. In order to lead in this regard, the manager should seek to build up that effort with some simple activities.

Firstly, it is important to define and communicate the principles, the values and ethics, according to which workers are expected to behave, and to develop as individuals. The process of defining, communicating and modeling those principles of behavior are initial steps toward the creation of a principled environment.

Tips for Creating a Code of Ethical Conduct

The manner in which the code is written, organized and presented will have an important impact on the degree to which employees will understand the code or refer back to it. Because an organization generally intends its code to be read by employees at different levels of responsibility and in a wide range of functional areas, the code should be written in plain, direct language. The syntax should be uncomplicated.

- Be clear about the objectives that the code is intended to accomplish.
- Get support and ideas for the code from all levels of the organization.
- Be aware of the latest developments in the laws and regulations that affect your industry.
- Write as simply and clearly as possible. Avoid legal jargon and empty generalities.
- Respond to real-life questions and situations.
- Provide resources for further information and guidance.
- In all its forms, make it user-friendly because ultimately a code fails if it is not used.

-- www.ethics.org

Next, it is important for the management to help codify that conduct. The creation of a code of ethics will help to clarify the expectations on the job, and help eliminate the poor, individual choices that can be made when people are left to their own discretion.

Finally, principled conduct must be taught! You will never be able to think up and codify all of the various challenges to principled behavior that will arise within the course of the work that must be done. People—that is, yourself and your workers—will always be plunged into situations in which decisions must be made but wherein manuals will not be around to consult. Even if they were, they would not cover each, identical situation. The objective, therefore, is not simply to create documents of rules base on intended values. The goal is to get the values imbedded into the minds of workers, thereby being translated into the work that they perform. Workers must be challenged to think consistently in terms of ethical, principled behavior.

In order to help achieve that goal, the manager should have in place some kinds of mechanisms to help fortify the effort. Training sessions—both formal and informal—should be instituted to make the ethical point central and valid to the employees. If they know it is important to you, it will be translated into importance for them. You will better your own position by modeling ethical behavior, and you will improve your workers by challenging them to do the same.

The work requires workers.

Managing the work environment is ultimately about the people who are working there. Every office, every production plant, has its informal, but recognized, hierarchies and controls. Getting things done is often as much about choosing the people as it is about choosing the procedure. It is knowing who can get things done, when, where and how. *Observation* is the key. The careful manager will look to see what is going on, with and through whom, and how it all takes place.

In accordance with this, we would suggest that there are at least three categories with which you should make yourself aware, if indeed you are planning to succeed within your organization: *the environment, the people and the actions taking place around you.*

Before you begin your assessment, however, you are going to have to settle the fact that, if indeed you are going to succeed, you are going to be required not only to *know*, but in some degree to *play*, the political game at the office. We can all be principled, and must be. But this does not preclude the fact that savvy is also a requisite for accomplished management. As our coach resounded in an earlier section, "You must know your players." Now we contend that you must not only know your players, but you must also know the opposing team, the game and the venue in which the game is going to be played. You can be *principled*, and in this respect, *political* at the same time! They are not opposing characteristics, but rather complimentary, if indeed we act wisely. The motive is not short cuts and one-upmanship, but effectiveness and efficiency.

How formally or not you may wish to address these concerns for yourself is up to you. Management gurus may suggest that documenting, charting and practically codifying your approach to these matters is wise.

Others may say, not at all. We contend that they are important enough factors to address, and therefore items with which the manager, or would-be manager, should be more than marginally acquainted.

1. **Observe the environment**. It may not be true in the office space that "any question is a good question," yet it is true that asking the right questions is certainly an effective tool. In order to find your way through the maze of office politics, carefully place questions to your coworkers to discern the best practices. *Concentrate, however, on processes and procedures, not on personalities.* Let the "people information" come to you, do not pursue it. Tactful, purposeful questions may degenerate into office gossip if you are not careful. And gossip is the last behavior that you want to model as a manager.

   Further, sit back and stealthily watch what is taking place around you. Key questions apply. Who are the people that are actually getting things done? Who are the people that they associate with in the office? What actions allow them to get the things done that they do? What are the rewards and what are the disciplines that result when various actions are involved? Who are the recipients of the most of each? What is the overall manner in which people interact within the office? Friendly or aloof? Relaxed or very structured? Formal or rather informal? A manager may be well served to create such a list of tactful questions and then begin to systematically gather answers, especially within the early days, thereby acclimating himself to the relationships of people and processes that are in play.

Making mental notes—and taking time to recognize these factors at the office in the first place—will go a long way to make the path to success straight and accessible, both for you and for the people with whom you work.

2. **Observe the people**. So who *are* the people that are making things happen? In every area of your work life, whether dealing with those who are supervisors over you, or employees who answer to you, there will be key people who will make the access that you need available, and the work that you need completed finished for you. Knowing throughout the organization (and not only within your immediate section) who those people are, is crucial to your success.

   Remember, too, that it is not always the most visible or obvious people that meet this requirement. Sometimes access to an administrative secretary can be much more instrumental than access to his boss. The point is not to know the "somebody's", but to know the persons who really make work happen: the power behind the people. Who is always sought for advice? What names come up most often as the do-ers? Who holds the real keys of access to the most important decision makers? Who are killing time, and who are using time to make a killing? Be sensible and insightful as you examine the real team at work around you.

3. **Observe the actions**. Just as the people working for you will look to your *behavior* to interpret the real expectations of their actions, so you need to be observing the actions of those around you to help

interpret what is really going on. Reports, emails and inter-office memos can fly. Many things can be said. But the real communication is enshrined in what the responses are to the communication that takes place. When you are receiving communications from within the company—from both above and below your pay grade— look to see what actions have preceded, accompanied, and then finally resulted from the communication that you have received. In this essence, actions do speak louder than words.

> **"Be as shrewd as snakes and as innocent as doves."**
>
> **-- Jesus of Nazareth**

The wise observer can help himself by so carefully construing the environment. He should pay special attention to:

- **Never allow answers to be less than reasonable.** If there is the appearance that information has been somehow left out, or that there should be more to the story than what has been delivered to you, seek as much information as necessary to clarify. Do so through more than one source, and ask the questions in various ways to see if answers are altered or fail to match.

- **Be cordial with everyone**. As much as possible, show interest and affinity with everyone that you can. People are more likely to share information with those who do not threaten them, or by whom they do not feel judged. When people offer information, take it seriously, without jumping to conclusions. With peers, involve yourself with them in both internal and external activities as much as you can, within reason for your lifestyle concerns. With subordinates, caution the amount of familiarity that is appropriate for your position and work environment, but take measures to instill the sense of connection and collaboration that has been so expressed in this book.

- **Build a network**. This is very near to the above, but takes the concept a step further. In any political environment— and your office is one— you will find that increasing the number of allies available to you will be indispensable. Yet keep this in mind: they are not only allies. They are friends. Collaborators. *People.* The more you show true affection and concern for those working alongside you, the more they will believe in that affinity and respond to it (as they should, because it is genuine!). Being available to share information, when appropriate; willing to show the new person around and incorporate them into everything possible; able to address the concerns of coworkers; bold to approach the bosses appropriately, etc.; will only go toward establishing your credibility, leadership and authority throughout the organization. That, in turn, will build your loyalty base, and your ability to obtain help in return.

- **Be supportive to all**. Sometimes, we are inclined only to be helpful to those who are our superiors, from whom we perceive there can be advantage resulting from such behavior. The wise office manager will be available to help any and all that he can provide with the necessary assistance. When you are helping others to achieve in their own right, it results in returns that can not always be preconceived, or at times even identified. But helpfulness is a powerful tool! Within the boundaries of what is allowed, and available within the company to be given according to your influence or power, be generous in sharing such capital.

- **Be appropriate** in all situations. This might sound odd, but it is a simple rule of good conduct. There are times and places to express certain behaviors with coworkers. But there are rarely times to be too loose, and never times to be unaware and lacking in tact. The loud mouth at social functions will be loath to receive additional trust from either supervisors or subordinates. Even in informal, social settings, the careful manager will remember that he or she is always on display, and at the end of the day, will be judged at work on the basis of conduct both at and away from work! Whether at staff gatherings, company social affairs, weekends at the boss', or wherever, the wise manager will always exhibit conduct within the values and guidelines of the corporation, always aware of the need (and mandate!) for respect.

The fact will always be that office politics will not go way. The political process will not disappear and leave you alone. It will be a part of your business life, and a reality of your every day experience, should you choose to pursue a career in the management of people and business. On the other hand, it need not be the end of hope.

Here is wise advice. If the politics of your office are so severe, so intense, and so pervasive as to make your experience dreadful or demeaning, then find other work. Or at least, find another place to do your work. Frankly, too much is too much. We are not contending that success is available to you only through the pursuit of top-dog, political maneuvering. If that is the case, then as an ethical and thoughtful person, you are in the wrong place. Too much is too much. Period. Life is not meant to be a rat race, or an abusive pursuit to be king of the hill. On the other hand, some element of the wise handling of people and circumstances is necessary. As long as people are people, you can not avoid the necessity of becoming a handler of people. A politician in the marketplace. Not in the negative connotations of the word, but in the elements of having to learn to deal with your environment, and to shape it to your advantages; which, as a good manager, should coincide with the advantage of the company, and the workers, who are investing in its success!

It would be great if everyone behaved appropriately at all times, and that all conduct was only altruistic in nature. Alas, you must be more wise than that! You must be able to navigate the minefields of the office, and cover them with care.

The work requires disciplined workers.

This implies that an eye must be kept not only upon the individual worker, but upon the work force as a whole. One of the least appealing duties of the manager is that of employee discipline. Taking action when employees are unable or unwilling to perform, or when the attitudes of an employee bring conflict into the team as a whole, then the competent manager has to be ready and able to perform his duty.

Grace is an admirable, and necessary, character trait for the modern supervisor. People are people, and especially creative people may come with a litany of quirks and oddities. These are not really items for concern. The manager may need to coordinate work teams and office arrangements around some of these inconveniences, but largely they should not challenge the performance of the group. Wisdom in balancing the needs of the organization with that of individual workers will be a grand assistance, and a noble pursuit.

When is the manager compelled to invoke disciplinary measures? Simply put, *when the performance of the worker is adversely affecting the productivity and healthy operation of the team or organization.* When other workers are consistently left to carry increased burdens and workloads because of the deficiencies of the individual, then the manager must step in to bring correction.

Discipline in the work place need not be completely about confrontation and punishment, however. In fact, *discipline should be first about dealing positively with situations, and bringing the necessary guidance and instruction to help an employee return to proper behavior and performance.* This can be achieved when the manager keeps in mind certain factors that contribute to the healthy use of discipline.

Most employees will not despise correction, when it comes in the form of helpful instruction and constructive criticism. The majority of workers want to do their job well, and appreciate the "heads-up" that allows them to do so. The reverse side is true as well. Productive employees that perceive that a lack of discipline is evident in the work place are less likely to appreciate the overall management situation, and to have less faith in the system that they serve. It might create a sense of irreverence for the good work that takes place as it is contributed by healthy performers.

Discipline that is applied up front and early, as opposed to that which waits for small issues to balloon into major problems, is much more affective. Action should be taken as close to the time as possible in which infractions have occurred. Problems left to fester can escalate into much larger dilemmas, and what often could have been corrected as minor infractions grow to the place that they require much grander forms of disciplinary action. Additionally, the manager who seeks to avoid confrontation (for whatever reason) stands to leave situations to fester in this way. The excuse, "I'll leave it alone and see if it works itself out," so often used to justify inaction is likely to be misinterpreted as a lack of care about a certain action or situation. Again, small items are in danger of becoming much larger issues in this scenario.

Evaluation of employee behavior must be based on performance, not on issues of personality. When company policies and procedures are well communicated, then documented and shared with employees, the standard of evaluation is made clear. This rule must be clear for two reasons.

1. The manager is inevitably going to run up against people that, for a variety of reasons, exhibit behavior that is less than pleasant or appropriate. It may be due to temporary, personal issues, or it may be due to much more ingrained traits. Still, if that behavior

is not bringing detriment to performance, disrupting the behavior of other workers or in some form violating the values and goals of the organization, then patience is required.

2. Sometimes behavior that is exhibited for "acceptable" reasons of hardship in the personal or professional life qualifies for an element of compassion. Remember, management is about *people*, and not just the work, and therefore demands oversight that can creatively work with, and work to compensate for, temporary situations growing out of such unfortunate scenarios. In the end, however, the manager does not have the option of allowing job performance and organizational productivity to be consistently compromised by such behavior. Providing help to overcome temporary difficulties is admirable, and necessary. Covering persistent, sub-par performance is ultimately detrimental to the good of the company, as well as of that individual. Job performance must be the qualifying factor when determining the use (or non-use) of discipline.

Discipline must be fair and consistent in usage. While it is true that real problems of behavior or attitude must be addressed early, it should also be said that a quality manager will not take action without understanding the situation well. Cursory investigations or snap judgments will serve no one well. Decisions to discipline a particular employee for misconduct that are not met with equal treatment in other times and places, or with other employees, will undermine authority and trust. And while each person is an individual, the tailoring of decisions should be left to *rewards*, and not to the area of *disciplines*. In other words, different employees may respond to different forms of reward. Differentiation in the use of discipline, however, is perceived as favoritism, not as insightful care on the part of the manager. And while a manager may indeed have different levels of relationship with different employees, when in the work place, and when dealing with work issues, there can be no issues of favoritism. The temptation to cover for a friend must be resisted for the integrity of the company and of the manager's position within the organization.

Coworkers must be held to account for their performance in the work place. The ideal manager is attentive to the issues and concerns of workers, while still maintaining an environment of disciplined behavior. He restricts his disciplinary decisions to issues of performance, and allows no one to escape responsibility when consistent actions *and attitudes* bring detriment to that performance.

Discipline (when done right) requires work.

Once it is clear that discipline is first about *help and encouragement,* and only when that fails is it about *punishment,* then the manager is ready to consider how discipline is done. The attitude of a good supervisor is focused on the assistance that is necessary to bring workers up to their greatest performance potential, and thereby to maximize productivity for the organization. It is not to be the headmaster or taskmaster of the work. It is to serve the efforts of the goals of the organization by serving the needs of the workers that contribute and invest in the accomplishment of those goals. Such an attitude, once embraced, will help the manager to prepare the environment of trust and concern that contributes positively toward those ends.

In compliance with this attitude, the manager is determined to bring only the form of discipline that best meets the given situation, and only to the degree that is necessary. This requires the executive to be informed, and following that, to be prepared in his dealings with his employees. He is averse to overreaction and is determined to bring about the best result possible, with the least negative fallout. Again, he is concerned more about correcting and helping than about punishing infractions. This may be termed *progressive* or *incremental discipline.*

It is important for the business or organization, as well as for the employees and the manager, to have as much of the disciplinary measures of the organization as possible outlined, codified and circulated. The more that people are aware of what to consider acceptable behavior and understand the results of violations, the more that excuses may be undermined. And the less are the chances of anyone being caught unaware. This is to the advantage of everyone involved.

> **"Discipline is the refining fire through which talent becomes ability."**
>
> **-- Roy L. Smith**

Although the processes in differing organizations will be modified to meet the specific needs and values of those organizations, some basics will generally apply. It should be stated as well that there are forms of discipline outside of the standard, codified systems within the organization that may also be useful, and of which you should certainly be aware. Let us consider some helpful guidelines.

1. Determine the *kind* of infraction that you are facing. Is it a **performance-based** issue (you are not getting the required work-related results), or is it a matter of **behavioral misconduct**? The first are more easily approached through standard performance evaluation procedures, whereas the second may be more delicate, and require a degree of care, especially when dealing with accusations and their results. (There may be legal advice required to handle certain situations as well.) Determine to what degree the infraction has been committed, its severity, what resources you need to handle it— including assistance from peers or higher management— and any other concerns for dealing with this specific situation.

2. Determine the steps that are available, either in the disciplinary procedures manual or other organizational documents available to you, or through considering the *progressive* options that are yours.

    a. **Speak**. This ranges from the comments that are made in passing to encourage certain performance results or changes in behavior, to more official settings in which face-to-face discussions are initiated, but which do not yet require more formal procedures. These times should be free enough to engender discussion and help the compliant employee to move on quickly and easily.

    b. **Write.** If behavior is persistent, or of enough importance from the outset, then you should put both the complaint and the guidance into written form. If it is important enough to document in writing, then it is important enough to document instructions and to have follow up discussions in which the employee is given opportunity to discuss the issues raised, and most importantly, to make plans together with the manager to move forward in compliance. (Many would suggest that written counsel should be given in person, in an office setting rather than elsewhere, and dealt with in that moment together.) *Anything written should be added to the employee's file* for safe keeping and follow up.

c. **Evaluate.** When verbal and written instructions go unheeded or do not result in acceptable improvement, then the next step is to formalize the evaluation and include it in either a performance review at a regularly scheduled time, or if necessary, in an extra review. As these performance evaluations are often looked over by higher levels of management, if there are any, this has the added weight of being passed along the chain of command. In the case of behavioral misconduct, this stage may not wait for performance evaluations, and therefore an official *reprimand* should be constructed and shared with higher management. Such evaluations must, of course, be in writing and added to the employee's permanent file.

d. **Demote or suspend**. When poor performance continues, then more drastic measures must be adopted. In the case of performance-based infractions, the next step is to demote, or at least move, the underperforming employee. As it is possible that an employee has simply been promoted or moved into a job of which he or she is simply not capable, it is worth the effort to examine the situation and see if there is not some parallel move that would be fitting of the skills and disposition that are involved. If not, then an actual demotion may be necessary to protect the good of the organization and the other workers.

In the event of behavioral misconduct, it may be necessary to suspend an employee at this point, removing him from the office before further damage is sustained, and allowing for time and space to bring repair to the work environment. (If such a step is required in the event of misconduct, then pay should be granted while a review of the situation ensues. If, however, it has already moved to the point of obvious, disciplinary concern, then suspension should be without pay.)

e. **Terminate.** When all steps have failed, then termination of employment may be the only remaining option. And it should be the *only* remaining option before implementation. By this step, you should have adequate documentation to prove that termination was both acceptable and essential. It is imperative for you to be aware of the hiring and firing guidelines of both your organization and regulatory agencies. As this is one of the most delicate, and severe, of the responsibilities facing you, it would be worth the time and effort to become informed and adept in this area. (Study more on the topic in our companion book, "The Greatest Resource: Human Resource Management".)

3. **Work *with* employees to improve performance and behavior.** We have addressed this throughout the book in various incarnations, but it is certainly worth voicing again at this point. In fact, we might consider it essential. The task of discipline must be about the advance of the company first, yes, but it is also about the partnership of the company, the management and the employee to bring about desired results.

As in everything we have addressed, communication is at the core of good, disciplinary proceedings, at whatever level. You want to be able to address workers and help them to understand what the problems are, what the results of the problems are, and what corrective measures are necessary for addressing them. Being so informed, everyone may move forward together toward better results.

When communicating with workers in this context, always begin by describing the behavior that has been deemed inappropriate or unacceptable. Help them to understand the impact that the behavior has on the team, the organization and on the individual. Outline what needs to be changed to proceed, and what the consequences of either compliance or non-compliance would be. Encourage the employee to know that all available help will be given to aid the situation, but make it clear that the employee must individually step up and take responsibility. At the end, unless it is a situation demanding immediate termination, it is appropriate to work together to determine a plan for improvement to which every side may be held accountable for implementation. Creating and enacting such an improvement plan, complete with stated goals, a schedule for accomplishment, and an outline of the essential resources and training required for a positive outcome, may save you from having to go through much more difficult, time consuming and costly measures further into the future.

The management of *people*, more than just work tasks or project outlines, is a sensitive affair. Yet, the manager today is being called upon more than ever to serve the purposes of coach, mentor, and guidance counselor. The necessary preparation for these tasks can not be overstated in the realm of management studies today.

> **"Take time to appreciate employees and they will reciprocate in a thousand ways. An employee's motivation is a direct result of the sum of interactions with his or her manager."**
>
> **-- Bob Nelson**

It begins in the mind and determination of the manager-to-be. Once you have determined that the people task is the priority engagement of your job; that motivating others to excel in their positions of responsibility, and delegating that responsibility effectively; that training and developing the human resources available to your team are vital to the objective set out before you; then, and really only then, are you ready to take on the job that is the manger's today.

Proper care of the work demands prudent care of the people that are involved in the work. Care of those people, alas, depends on yet another form of care: that of caring for oneself.

Chapter 5
Managing Yourself

As much as your ability to coordinate projects, formulate teams, coach workers and bring benefit to your organization are the marks of your effectiveness as a manager, none of these things will be *sustainable* if you are not also aware of the need to manage yourself. Personal care—mentally, emotionally, physically and spiritually—must be directly in focus if you are to be of value well into the future. In fact, if you are to do the job that you must do now, you must be taking measures to guard your own welfare, as much as the welfare of all of the people and the company you serve.

Those who are a part of your life, whether at or outside of work, are additionally affected by the choices that you make in this department. A person with the amount of responsibility that is required of your position is under a great deal of pressure to perform many functions, to do them in a timely fashion, and to produce great results for everyone involved. The work can become completely overwhelming, and you may find yourself swimming in a pond that seems to have no shores. You may find your relationships under stress, your health deteriorating, your family life disappearing, and your peace of mind gone from sight, unless you are willing to put some thought and effort into taking care of yourself.

Just as the employees working for you must feel appreciated, satisfied and fulfilled, you must be careful to contribute to those same concerns in your own life. There is not one part of the equation that will not be better served by the health and wholeness that you bring to the office when you are avoiding the pitfalls of overwork, stress and tunnel vision. You must be able to translate positive attitudes, enthusiasm and faith in the goals and processes in which you are collectively participating, and you can not do that if it has all been drained from you. The manager that is tired, unfocused, stressed out and on edge simply can not bring benefit to his environment. He can not inspire others to levels of achievement and productivity. In essence, he models defeat.

So, the care of self is ultimately the care of the organization and other workers. Self preparation yields others who are prepared. Self concern, in the positive sense, motivates others who will care for themselves, for those around them, and for the work that must be done. To neglect this aspect is injurious to your own life, and detrimental to the work that you perform.

Take a look at two areas of concern that might quickly cast their spells over your life if you are not careful and aware: *stress* and *overwork*.

DEALING WITH STRESS

One of the greatest killers of effectiveness in any organization is stress. It is unavoidable. No position of real responsibility is ever going to come without a level of intensity. Not everything in the work place is under your control—in fact, very little is—and so you will meet with situations beyond your ability to handle all of the details. The result: stress. All of the things that go into making companies run well and managers work effectively, as we have been discussing in this book, come with the back handed potential of less than perfect results. It will all conspire to generate many days when it feels as though the work is pregnant with problems.

Additionally, what occurs outside of the work place is bound to contribute to the situation. How many of us live lives that are devoid of stress? Essentially, none of us. But the people who have achieved levels of both personal and professional success are bound to be people with ever-increasing responsibilities and concerns. The relationships and circumstances that are a part of your life when you are away from work do not check themselves out at the door once you enter the office. That being said, all is not hopeless. Far from it. Stress management is simply another part of being effective in your job. If you know it is part and parcel of the work, then you can prepare for it, and have plans to overcome its effects.

Use this chart to help identify oncoming stress.

MENTAL STRESS

* Unable to concentrate
* Irritable/moody
* Avoid things
* Fear of danger
* Expect trouble
* Expect negative results
* Worry about grades
* Worry about others
* Worry about body

PHYSIOLOGICAL

BEHAVIORAL

* Nail biting
* Grinding teeth
* Disturbed sleep
* Avoidance
* Speech and/or coordi-
  nation difficulties
* Stuttering/rapid speech
* Weight changes
* Changes in eating habits

* Trembling	* Sweating
* Dizziness	* Fatigue
* Pounding heart	* Tense muscles
* Dry mouth and throat	* Headache
* Backache	* Sore neck/shoulders
* Queasy stomach	* Intestinal problems
* Trouble breathing	* Cold joints
* Frequent urination	

www.counseling.tcu.edu/stressindicators.htm

The reality is that stress is manageable. Inevitable, indeed, but still manageable. Let us turn our attention, then, to attitudes and actions that can help us to keep this animal caged. Start by understanding that it is your responsibility to do so. Your company may have helps, such as stress management courses or seminars, but in the end, no one is going to bring your mind and spirit into balance for you.

Personal responsibility begins by dealing with the issues of stress that you can manage yourself. There are things that you can do to relieve yourself from having to deal with undue stress that has mounted; or better still, to keep it from accumulating in your system from the beginning. Much of it, you will find, has to do with attitude. Get your mind into the proper frame, and the rest of you will follow.

1. **Learn to say no.** Stress is the number one killer for the busy person like you. You have been well aware of this principle for some time, you have heard it preached again and again, and yet you fail to put it into practice. You must come to realize that you simply can not do personally all that is asked of you and be captive to all that is crying out for your attention. You must learn to sift the wheat from the

chaff, and then to prioritize the items that really should stay on your agenda. As for the rest... cut it loose!

2. **Take care of your body**. As cliché as it may sound, a proper diet and exercise are large allies in your cause to be healthy and strong. The body that is conditioned is much more able to absorb the beating that stress inflicts on the body. Resisting the urge to fill your body with junk is not only a more healthy approach for the body. It can also do much for the pocket book.

3. **Learn to relax and enjoy.** Like plugging your cell phone into the charger, relaxation is an energy booster for both the body and the mind. When it is time for you to take breaks from the work, actually get away from it! Physically remove yourself from the normal environment of your work space, and find some mental and physical distance from it in order to take a breath. Be aware of the times that the work is becoming so intense or so demanding that your joy in the task is being drained. Take steps to enjoy the people and the place in which you are going to spend the largest portion of your adult life! Sharing an occasional (tasteful!) joke and having a laugh with coworkers will go a great distance to making their days, and your own, pass more pleasantly and purposefully. (If you don't know any jokes, find a good website and borrow one occasionally.)

4. **Be in charge of your own schedule**. Do not let your schedule manage you. When meetings and events are optional, see how they fit with your

purposes. Do not just jump in to every opportunity. Use whatever organizational tools work best for you to keep yourself structured and on track. Refuse to be a victim of constant interruptions and phone calls. Becoming a slave to the tools of the business keeps *you* from being the manager of the resources and tools themselves. You are there to oversee them, not the opposite! Learn to appropriately combine events when feasible, and to eliminate duplicate efforts from your own schedule, and that of others. Simplify, simplify, simplify!

5. **Think positively, act positively**. More than a simple phrase that has been thrown around endlessly, this is an imperative for bringing your own thoughts in line, and to letting that spill over to other workers who are affected by you. You must learn to work out of your own abundance of energy and expectation. Learning is twenty percent information and eighty percent impartation, and the positive spirit that you are imparting to others, because it is inherent in you, will go far in lightening the load.

6. **Adapt to change.** Some things will never be within your ability to control, but they need not make you crazy. Learning to harness the process of change is an essential in today's society and marketplace. It is not unique to you to have to handle it, and the more that you can train yourself not to be thrown by change, the further ahead of the crowd you can remain. And the less flustered you will be in the process.

7. **Avoid the "Messiah" complex.** For all of the gifts, talents and accomplishments that you have brought

to the corporation, the fact remains that you are not the savior of everything around you. Given your absence or removal, things would probably continue. Perhaps even advance admirably. It is not your job to do it all, and it certainly is not your job to do everyone else's job. Believing yourself to be the center of the office/universe can lead to some nasty reckonings.

8. **Avoid being the victim, or the martyr.** When things do not go your way, as they are bound to do at times, you must decide what your response is to be. A victim is a person who has been overcome by circumstance. Today's environment demands that you be an overcomer of circumstances. The martyr, on the other hand, is not only a victim, but a willing victim. A victim by choice. Again, it is about attitude. When adversity comes, will you immediately allow your mind to occupy that hurt space that insists upon reminding you that you are not properly appreciated? Or, will you use it as an incentive to have even more to offer the next time around. The business world is littered with victims who failed to turn setbacks into advantages. They are the ones who could not control their anger or disappointment. Those who let the situation defeat the spirit. Such a person is bound to meet with great bouts with stress.

Stress is indeed going to confront you as you seek to manage the many aspects of life and work that are given into your capable hands. Learning to take the initiative in dealing with that stress will be a key to advancing your cause of being the best manager possible: at the office, and at home.

BALANCING WORK

The more capable that you prove to be, and the more that ability is recognized, the greater the demands will be on your time and attention as responsibility is shifted into your hands. More responsibility means more activity. More activity means more time. And all of it adds up to the fact that you are in danger of being swallowed up by the workload.

We discussed in an earlier chapter that, in many work environments today, poor effort and bad results are often rewarded in ways that we do not always recognize. Workloads are shifted, assignments are delegated out to be followed up or redone, and the incompetent one goes about his business while everyone works to clean up his mess. Incompetence is rewarded, while the capable ones are handed more to do.

The fact is that every organization in the world wants to work with the best people possible. No one wants to deal with duplicate efforts and needless errors. When that capable, effective person is located, she is launched into positions where her can-do attitude and gifted responses bring about great results. The demands build up, and her desires to please and to produce propel her into an ever increasing number of goals. Soon, she is a victim of her own competence, swallowed up in the flood of demands and expectations. She takes no time off, and when she does, takes a stack of work with her. Her home is a second office. Her computer keeps her attached like and umbilical cord, even when she is on vacation. And sickness has never stopped her from staying plugged into things at work, no matter what the doctor says.

Write this down: ***good management requires hard work***. No one is going to downplay that fact. In order to achieve, there is a price to pay. To whom much is given, much is required. The one from which much is required requires much time in order to get it done. It is the reality. That fact, however, is not the total of your life. There is, indeed, more to life than work. It is in the balance of work and other aspects of life that you will find purpose, satisfaction and fulfillment. That, again, will return itself to the work in the form of the person with greater equilibrium, greater stability. It is proven that such employees (and managers!) contribute in higher returns to the productivity and environment of healthy companies.

> **"Normal day, let me be aware of the treasure you are. Let me learn from you, love you, savor you, bless you before you depart. Let me not pass you by in quest of some rare and perfect tomorrow. Let me hold you while I may, for it will not always be so. One day I shall...bury my face in the pillow, or raise my hands to the sky, and want, more than all the world your return."**
>
> **-- Mary Jean Irion**

Do a personal inventory. How much of your life is dictated by your work? How controlled are you by the office, even when you are not there? How is that affecting your personal relationships? What does it mean to your time to be involved in other activities or organizations? What has it done to your volunteer time for community events or religious services? Is your husband, your wife or your children inclined to treat you as a stranger? Do you feel lost anywhere except at your desk?

If so, you have some work to do to bring some balance to your job and to your life. (By the way, chances are that, if this is your experience, then that of your employees is not very far off! It is something to keep in mind.) Begin by examining yourself: *your mind, your actions and your attitude.*

- **Your mind**. Do you find yourself talking about your own work everywhere you go, even in social settings? Does work invade your sleep in the form of dreams, or wake you in the midnight hours?

- **Your actions.** They speak louder than words, you know. Are you glued to the office, getting there early and leaving late *every day*? Do you rarely go on vacation, or do you cut vacations short to return to the office? Have your days off found you coming by "just to check in", or to "get a couple of things done?" Do you work more than 48 hours per week *consistently*? Do you skip lunches and breaks, or take them in your office so that you can continue to work?

- **Your attitude.** Are you convinced that these issues above, while potentially important for other people, do not necessarily apply to you? Do you refuse to recognize the warning signs, even when pointed out to you by other people?

Each of these questions, and their answers, can lead you to an understanding about your position as a leader and manager. Because they indicate an imbalance in your own lifestyle, they will also become instructional to the people who are a part of your life, both at work and at home. *The choices that you make are themselves teachers.* They teach people about your priorities and expectations. They cause people to formulate opinions about you, and about the ways that they significantly, or rather insignificantly, fit into your life-picture. They teach what is expected of them in order to effectively match up to you.

There is plenty of room to work hard and still make sure that work is not your life. Even in the more caustic settings of non-profit and non-governmental agencies, where life and work so often become passionately intertwined, there is more to life than what takes place at the office. I have often heard, and even used myself, the phrase, "My work is not what I do; it is who I am." And there can be some real truth to that statement in many positions of leadership. Yet there are ways to "be" what that life-cause requires without it all being attached with that umbilical cord to your desk.

If you characteristically fit into any of the above scenarios, or if you are planning to enter a career soon with all of the flare and passion you can muster, take these helps into account now. Be a possessor and a model of balance, and you will go far to encourage peace, pleasantness and productivity in your work place, in your own life, and in the lives of the people attached to you and to the workers who labor together with you. Everyone then wins. Consider these ways to help you bring balance to your situation.

1. **Work less.** Commit to a reasonable work week, and then hold yourself accountable to it as much as possible. Other than in exceptional circumstances (and be honest and reasonable with your definition of "exceptional), set a departure time from the office

daily, and do it. Leave the stacks behind. If you can not do this on your own, then make a daily schedule with another person that holds you accountable, such as trips together to the gym at the end of the workday, or a regular coffee meet-up with your spouse.

2. **Leave the office at the office.** When you go home or out with friends, or even colleagues, make it a point not to speak of work. A little banter at the dinner table to answer, "How was your day?" is not a bad thing. But endless conversations about the work, workers, bosses, customers, etc., will add nothing to your social life. The stacks of papers should be left neatly on the desk. Unless something severe is impending, do not take your work home with you. It will be there when you arrive tomorrow.

3. **Expand your social network**. Make sure that all of your relationships are not centered around work. This will assist greatly your efforts at numbers one and two above.

4. **Exercise**. We have said it before, but a routine of exercise brings more than one kind of strength to your body. The chemical reactions brought on by exercise are proven stress-relievers, as well as mind and energy motivators. Bodily strength helps to combat fatigue, both in the body and the mind.

5. **Take vacations that are really vacations**. This is really self-explanatory, but still must be said. Vacations should not include cell phone and computer links to the office. There is no such thing as a "working vacation". Leave such absurd notions behind, and go have some fun and relaxation!

FOREVER LEARNING

> **"I am learning all the time. The tombstone will be my diploma."**
> -- Eartha Kitt

One of the absolute must-do's in the realm of self-management is this: *never stop learning*. Your edge will only remain as sharp as the attention you give to keeping it sharp, and learning is the tool that brings that about. As a person, and as a professional, there will always be things to discover that add to your excellence. Developing a plan, as systematic as possible, for reading and study can not be overemphasized as an essential component of your potential success.

On the personal side (although it is difficult in this regard to separate the personal and professional, as the two will converge at many points), it is helpful to take a few easy steps:

1. **Read**. Shut down the television and DVD, and pick up a book. Subscribe to or occasionally pick up a periodical relating to a subject that you enjoy that is not directly related to work. The process of reading is as important as the information that you are gathering. It works to keep you mentally sharp and constantly in growth stages.

2. **Involve yourself in non-work related organizations or associations.** Find something that you like to do, or feel compelled to be a part of, and contribute some time and energy to it. The people that you will come into contact with, the

methods and strategies used outside of your own professional environment, and the experiences that will become a part of your life will serve only to enrich you.

> **"Man's mind, once stretched by a new idea, never regains its original dimensions."**
> -- Oliver Wendell Holmes

3. **Make time for solitude**. Learning is not always about verbal or written interaction. Making time to be still and to allow the thoughts of life swirl through the mind and to gradually take coherent and cohesive forms is a surprisingly constructive task. The busyness of life today is such that people rarely engage the art of reflection anymore. Find a favorite and engaging spot. A park, a beach, a mountaintop or your favorite chair in the den. Separate yourself from everything and everyone for some designated moments, and let your thoughts be your partner in communication.

4. **Engage your faith**. It is important to desegregate the weekend mindset from the weekday one that most people experience today. Faith and religion, if a person embraces them, are not well served—nor is the person possessing them—when they are separated from the affairs of a person throughout the course of daily routines. This dichotomy is neither good for the soul nor the mind, as it creates conflicts of conscience, and may lead to contradictions in thoughts and actions that confuse the unseen, inner parts. Wholeness can not be a reality when such divisions exist within the person's own psyche. Faith is about hope and expectation, which can help lead

to attitudes compliant with these characteristics. By embracing and engaging your faith, you can bring the so-called "secular" and the "sacred" together into a package that serves you as a person, and serves those around you who are touched by your actions.

This process of life long learning that we describe here is made even more pertinent by professional needs. Professions are constantly being challenged, changed and energized by new concepts. Admittedly, some of these are little worth keeping, and will pass in a short time. These are fads of the business (although, even fads can bring helpful hints and instructions). But others will actually conspire to transform the face of the industry you work in. It is imperative to keep sharp and alert through constant interaction with the developments in your area of expertise.

Beyond that, the model that you set as a life long learner will have effects on those working with you. As you are staying aware, they will be challenged to do the same. As you bring new and constructive ideas into the work place, others will be inspired to creativity themselves. Learning is a positive symptom of a healthy work place, and like many symptoms, can be contagious.

It is said that knowledge is increasing at such a pace that the techniques and tools required to do the job adequately change in only two or three years. If your knowledge and skills are remaining steadfast at the point they were when you entered your profession, then you are bound to be left behind in less than half of a decade. Those who are younger, hungrier and better equipped with the latest tools are just waiting to be discovered. And you, my friend, are waiting to be replaced. It does not take decades anymore to be relegated to the heap of the irrelevant, if time, technology and technique are left unattended.

The days of going to school, completing a solid degree, entering the work force and holding your space for decades have passed. It is an old model. Upper management positions are not held on the basis of seniority and longevity anymore. The "learning years" are no longer replaced by the "earning years." The two will likely become more integrated and synthesized in the years ahead. In order to keep pace, and more, to succeed, you will have to embrace an attitude (and a joy!) of life long learning.

The more training that you receive, the more that your mind is stretched to grapple with and tackle issues and ideas, then the more prepared that you are to bring positive qualities to your job. The better you will become at problem solving, motivation, evaluation and the development of others. As you are able to bring these qualities to the task, you will be increasingly rewarded for your effort, both personally and professionally, in the process. Some tips to the wise follow.

1. **Be attentive to personal development**. Begin by creating a *personal development plan*. Most people give thought to these *kinds* of things, but rarely take the time and apply the effort to actually formalize their thoughts and put them on paper. Take the time. You deserve it. (See the Addendum, "Creating a Personal Development Plan" for assistance.) Just doing so proves your commitment and intent to attain the highest level of performance.

2. **Read books for professional enrichment.** As in the personal realm, one of the easiest and most profound ways to stay sharp, learn new ideas and engage progress is through reading. Take note, however, that the amount of reading produced in any given field is growing, and much of it is "fluff". Try to avoid getting pulled into every new idea, and concentrate on items of substance. Trade magazines or journals, websites, etc., will be good sources for finding out what is available, and what is useful. (You can find a number of good ones referenced in the bibliography and works cited page and the end of this book.)

3. **Attend conferences and seminars.** When it actually meets your goals and objectives, look into the professional learning opportunities that exist. Examine the content of any such event prior to making the decision to attend, and make sure that it is worth your time, energy and resources.

4. **Visit other parallel organizations.** When it is possible and open to you, go and take a look at what others are doing to achieve results. Some companies actually make formal opportunities to see what is working within their organizations. As you create relationships, utilize them (carefully and appropriately) to cross pollinate and learn. See what programs they are using. Find out what changes have been implemented, and worked, and which have been ultimately rejected.

5. **Talk with mentors and peers**. Whether within the same organization, or outside, organize time to speak with others that might have information and

instruction to offer you. Be careful, however, not to organize time under the pretenses of personal visits, and then steer them toward more business-oriented engagements. This can be resented!

There are certainly other activities that can add to your learning experience, including professional and life long learning courses and other programs. These are often formulated for professional development and offered within organizations themselves. There are many ways to learn, and there is a lot of material available to help you in your quest. Find the tools that are useful and relevant to you, and put them into practice.

> **"Learning is a treasure that will follow its owner everywhere."**
>
> **-- Chinese Proverb**

USING A PERSONAL DEVELOPMENT PROGRAM

The creation of a personal development program is often stunted because of the person's perception that it must be a complex and overwhelming process. Our attempt here is to outline a process that is neither.

Good planning will help you to move toward better performance, as you learn to use your time, resources and tools effectively. You should begin with a thoughtful review of your desires for career, the organization of which you are now a part, and the ways in which the two coincide. If you have no plans or perceptions, then that is certainly the place to begin! If your plans and those of the company do not match, then you have some other decisions to make prior to beginning the career planning that is associated with this developmental process. Begin by knowing something of who you are, where you are planning to go, and who you are planning to work with in that process.

Use this outline beginning on the next page to help you in your planning process. Take a notebook, or sit down at your computer, and begin to formulate a draft of answers to these categories and questions regarding your own expectations, those of your place of work and the people involved there, and the way in which these all intersect to compose your work life and atmosphere.

> **"The basis of a good Personal Development Plan (PDP) is establishing a solid understanding of, where we have come from? Where we are now? Where do we need to go? This applies to the organization, the management team and each individual. Your PDP and that of your managers should all be aligned to the overall strategy and objectives for your organization as well as your personal goals, aspirations and values." - Unknown**

SECTION ONE: Personal Planning

What are my career plans? How are they intertwined with my place of employment?

1. What is the business that I am in? Is this where I intend to be?

2. Is this the business that the organization is truly attempting to create, or is there a distance to go? Are we on track?

> The answers to these first two questions will help you later as you determine the knowledge, skills and behavior necessary for your professional advance.

3. Is the structure of the organization prepared to achieve, or at least adequately pursue, the corporate goals?

   a. Are resources delegated to the stated priorities?
   b. Is the flow of information built around those priorities and the key functions for achieving them?
   c. Is the "bench" deep enough to achieve in the absence of particular players?
   d. Are lines of authority and roles of responsibility well defined?
   e. Is the communication process well established and functional within the organization?

> What is essentially being asked in this section is whether or not the organization's stated destination is being met by action. Is the balance of resources with work load up to the task?

4. Is this all heading in a direction that I want to go?

SECTION TWO: Personal Review

How do I currently match up to my goals, and my environment?

> "Converse with almost any man grown old in a profession, and you will find him regretting that he did not enter into some different course, to which he too late finds his genius better adapted, or in which he finds that wealth and honor are more easily attained."
>
> - Samuel Johnson

1. What are my strengths and weaknesses?

   > Note: You may want to get some outside help and opinion in this regard. If you have performance evaluations at your disposal, use those. Speak to family or friends. Get as open and honest an answer to this question as possible.

2. Which of my strengths can I best maximize to work toward my goals?

3. Which of my weaknesses do I have the capacity, through training and education, to strengthen or overcome? Which of them am I not likely to change too much, as it is not worth the effort and resources necessary to do so?

4. In what parts of my job have I demonstrated aptitude?

5. In what parts have I struggled? Have I struggled to the point of unacceptable?

6. Which areas of my job do I enjoy and feel comfortable with?

7. In which areas have I noticeably improved over the last year?

8. What have I attempted to improve over the last year that has not yielded much progress?

SECTION THREE: Personal Plan

What is necessary in order to move forward from where I am now, and where we are as an organization, to where I (we) plan to be?

1. What personal skills do I need to work on in the areas of management skills, relationship building, communication, attitude and presence, etc.?

2. What professional tools do I need to acquire or enhance in order to improve my performance? What areas of training do I need? How might I better be served with coaching or mentoring?

3. What new developments in my area of expertise do I need to become acquainted with? Highly competent in?

4. What are my options for obtaining the tools and resources that I need to excel?

> **Remember: Learning is more than acquiring knowledge. It is the application of knowledge! Your goal is to obtain better skills, which lead to higher performance opportunities and outcomes.**

There are basically three areas of concentration on which you may focus to find the help that you need.

a. **Education**: This is usually a very involved and broad pursuit that is designed for some formal accreditation or recognition. It will involve many subjects and prepare you for the bigger picture of your areas of pursuit.

b. **Training**: These programs are designed for more specific learning in order to acquire certain skills or detailed learning. Training may come through short courses, conferences, seminars, mentoring or a variety of other ways.

c. **Experience**: This is, after all, the great teacher. This could be done by simply taking on a task and "going for it", or by partnering with others to receive the experience in a combination with training. Experience that is coupled with one of the above options is more agreeable, and usually more productive.

5. How shall I then proceed?

a. Now ask: Through which of these methods might I get the help, guidance and development that I need to proceed?

b. Remember: there are costs in terms of time, energy and resources that must be committed to obtaining the help that you need. Take the cost into consideration.

c. Determine: What then, in result for investment, is my best option to obtain this help?

SECTION FOUR: Personal Action

What will I do with the answers and information that I have compiled in this review?

This chart can be utilized to put your answers together to formulate your Personal Development Plan. Be brief and concise.

Name:	Job Title:
Years with the organization: _____ **Term in present position:** _____ _____	**How do I perceive the direction of the organization and my personal involvement?**
List your formal job qualifications: _____ _____ _____ **Performance Review: How did you perform over the last year?**	**What were my major work-related achievements?** **What are my most evident weaknesses?**

	What are my most evident strengths?		
I should concentrate development in these areas:			
My major achievement objectives for the next year are:			
My dominant career interests are:			
To pursue my development objectives, I will complete the following:	**ACTION TO COMPLETE:**	**FINISH DATE:**	**ACCOUNTABLE TO:**

Concluding Thought

Once you have all of the knowledge and tools required to enter into your career in organizational management, you still remain only as ready as your attitude allows. When all is said and done, *it is not the knowing that counts, but the doing.*

For the person planning to manage in today's work environment, the challenge is great. The amount of creativity that is brought to bear in the modern work place requires managers to keep up with the pace. "The leader with no followers is just out for a walk," some wise person has reminded us. Many managers today are strolling through the marketplace, unable to inspire and encourage workers to follow after them. They are just out for a walk.

Some might interject here that it is not required that the manager lead, just manage. Organize things, structure them and govern them. Let the "leaders" create the vision. Let them inspire the workers. It is the manager's job to make sure that *their* vision is implemented. The problem is, that is old school, and no longer holds true. Not in the places where things are happening, and not with the people that are making it happen.

Today, management is about *people*. It is about teamwork, and therefore the coordination of teams. It is about personalities, and the quirks that accompany them. It is about coaching and encouraging, guiding and counseling, training and, yes, leading. Much is required of the modern manager, as organizations learn that "flat" models of organization work better than pyramids or ladders. The reduction in middle management is not driving the middle managers lower on the chain, but higher. And the number of them is being reduced to meet the expectations of better performance that are promised from these new models. The manager of today is indeed required to be visionary, to be organizational, to be motivational and to be productive!

Such is the challenge that you have chosen. The challenge to lead people, inspire productivity, encourage development of the organization and the people, and ultimately to enhance the bottom line of the company! Are you ready for that challenge?

Then you, my friend, are ready to begin to manage!

> **"There are two tragedies in a man's life. One is not having reached one's goal and the other is having reached it."**
> **-- Friedrich Nietzsche**
>
> **"Quality is not an act. It is a habit."**
> **-- Aristotle**
>
> **"He who rules his spirit has won a greater victory than the taking of a city."**
> **-- Jesus of Nazareth**

Afterword

It serves us well to note that, from beginning to end, our approach to management and all of its related fields is buttressed by a simple truth: we are informed by our faith. Throughout the text, we have endeavored to expound principles which are in line with our understanding of Christian life and conduct. We trust that this would not be off-putting to you! We have made no effort to preach to you, and there is no appeal to conversion in these pages, as you have seen. We do contend, however, that the Christian life and ethic actually coincide with the best of management principles. The morality and instruction that is provided in a thorough understanding of the Christian faith is not only helpful, but embellishing of the best characteristics of a good manager.

Should you desire to know more of our perspectives on this matter, and the manner in which it can inform your personal life, your work place and the lives of others, please do not hesitate to contact us. We are available to you.

Contact:

EME
PO Box 73004
Ano Glyfada 16510
Greece

Tel. +30 210 9651346 Fax. +30 210 9644920
ememin@hol.gr

Bibliography and Works Cited

* Aburdene, Patricia and Naisbitt, John. <u>Megatrends for Women.</u> Villard Books. New York. 1992.

* Blanchard, Kenneth and Johnson, Spencer. <u>The One Minute Manager</u>. Morrow, 1982.

* Buckingham, Marcus and Coffman, Curt. <u>First, Break All the Rules: What the World's Greatest Managers Do Differently</u>. Simon & Schuster, 1999.

* Collins, James C. <u>Good to Great: Why Some Companies Make the Leap and Others Don't.</u> Collins, 2001.

* Collins, James C. and Porras, Jerry I. <u>Built to Last: Successful Habits of Visionary Companies</u>. HarperBusiness, 1994.

* Curtis, Keith. <u>From Management Goal Setting to Organizational Results: Transforming Strategies into Action</u>. Quorum Books, 1994.

* Drucker, Peter F. <u>Managing for Results</u>. Harper & Row, 1964.

* <u>http://www.ganttchart.org.</u>

* <u>http://dictionary.cambridge.org</u>. Cambridge University Press, 2006.

* <u>http://www. web.cba.neu.edu</u>. "The Importance of Effective Communication".

* <u>http://www.managementfirst.com</u>. Emerald Group Publishing, 2006.

- http://www.managementlearning.com. ManagementLearning.com, 2006.

- http:// www.nos.org.

- http://www.time-mangement-guide.com. Time Management Guide.com, 2002.

- http://www.jobhuntersbible.com. Richard N. Bolles, 2004.

- Schein, Edgar. Career Anchors: Discovering Your Real Values. Pfeiffer, 1985.

- Parsloe, Eric. The Manager as Coach and Mentor. Beekman Publishing, 2000.

- Clemmer, Jim. The Leader's Digest: Timeless Principles for Team and Organization Success. The Clemmer Group, 2003.